EYEWITNESS GUIDES

FARM

End-over-end
butter churn

Two-day-old piglets

Hay knife

"Clucket"
sheep bell

Potato fork

Jersey cow and crossbred
Jersey-British White calf

19th-century
seed drill

Gloucester
Old Spot sow

One-week-old chicks

FARM

Butter print

Written by
NED HALLEY

Photographed by
GEOFF BRIGHTLING

Brahma hen
and cock

DK

DORLING KINDERSLEY
London • New York • Stuttgart

Lifter for
parsnips
and other
root crops

Lifter for docks
and thistles

Butter print

Dartmoor sheep

Crossbred
Dartmoor-
Manx lambs

Buff
Orpington
cock

Common
pitchfork for
hay and corn

Plunger
butter
churn

DK

A DORLING KINDERSLEY BOOK

Project editors Caroline Beattie and David Pickering
Art editor Sharon Spencer
Managing editor Gillian Denton
Managing art editor Julia Harris
Researcher Céline Carez
Production Charlotte Trail
Picture research Cynthia Hole
Consultant Martin Collier
Additional photography Geoff Dann,
Peter Anderson, and Gary Ombler

This Eyewitness ® Guide has been conceived by
Dorling Kindersley Limited and Editions Gallimard

First published in Great Britain in 1996
by Dorling Kindersley Limited,
9 Henrietta Street, London WC2E 8PS

4 6 8 10 9 7 5

Copyright © 1996 Dorling Kindersley Limited, London

Visit us on the World Wide Web at
http://www.dk.com

A CIP catalogue record for this book is
available from the British Library.

ISBN 0 7513 6065 1

Colour reproduction by
Colourscan, Singapore
Printed in China
by Toppan Printing Co., (Shenzhen) Ltd.

Contents

Root cutter

6
The first farmers
8
Animal power
10
The tractor
12
The plough
14
Fields and soil
16
Sowing the seed
18
Protecting the crop
20
Harvesting by hand
22
Threshing and winnowing
24
Threshing by machine
26
Harvesting by machine
28
Wheat to bread
30
Favourite food
32
Maize and potatoes
34
Feeding the animals
36
Market gardening
38
Fruit farming

40
Farmhouse and farmyard
42
Barns and outbuildings
44
Dairy farming
46
Milk products
48
Cattle farming
50
Sheep farming
52
Sheep shearing
54
Goat farming
56
Pig farming
58
Chicken farming
60
Ducks and geese
62
The future of farming
64
Index

The first farmers

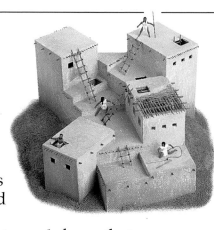

FARMING BEGAN more than 10,000 years ago in Turkey and the Middle East. It started with the discovery that certain grasses growing in the region produced edible seeds which could be planted to produce a new crop. (These grasses are now called cereals.) People began to clear and cultivate the ground for annual plantings of the grasses. They learned, too, to tame the cattle, goats, and sheep that roamed wild across the land. Herds were kept for their meat, milk, and skins, and tame animals bred from them. Unlike their hunter-gatherer ancestors, who had to move on when they had consumed all the plant and animal life around them, the new farmers stayed in one place and formed the first human settlements. Farming produced spare food, freeing more and more people from the daily struggle to find enough to eat. New activities, such as building houses and trading, became possible. Farming settlements were soon being established right across Asia, in Africa, and in the Americas. The history of human civilization had begun.

FARMING COMMUNITY
Wealth from farming made towns possible. Catal Huyuk in Turkey was one of the very first. By 6000 B.C. it had more than 1,000 houses, crowded together and entered by ladders through the roofs. Most of its people worked in agriculture, growing cereals and fruits, or raising livestock, but others made clothes, pottery, tools, and weapons, and traded them with the farmers for food.

MOVABLE FEAST
Ancient Egyptians were among the first farmers to produce food on a commercial scale, trading both within Egypt and internationally, by land and by sea. Here, grain from the harvest is being measured and the quantities recorded by scribes.

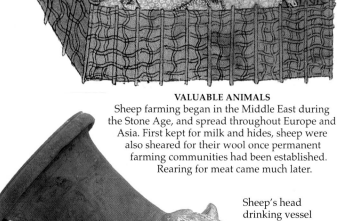

Sheep are being milked in a sheepfold in this 14th-century illustration

VALUABLE ANIMALS
Sheep farming began in the Middle East during the Stone Age, and spread throughout Europe and Asia. First kept for milk and hides, sheep were also sheared for their wool once permanent farming communities had been established. Rearing for meat came much later.

Sheep's head drinking vessel from ancient Greece

Emmer, the wheat most widely grown by ancient Greek and Roman farmers

CEREALS AND GRASS
Wheat, oats, barley, rice, maize, and millet were all originally wild grasses. Like other grasses that produce edible grain, they are known as cereals, or cereal grasses. In Britain, the most widely grown cereal of a region is known (in that region) as corn. In North America, Australia, and New Zealand, maize is called corn.

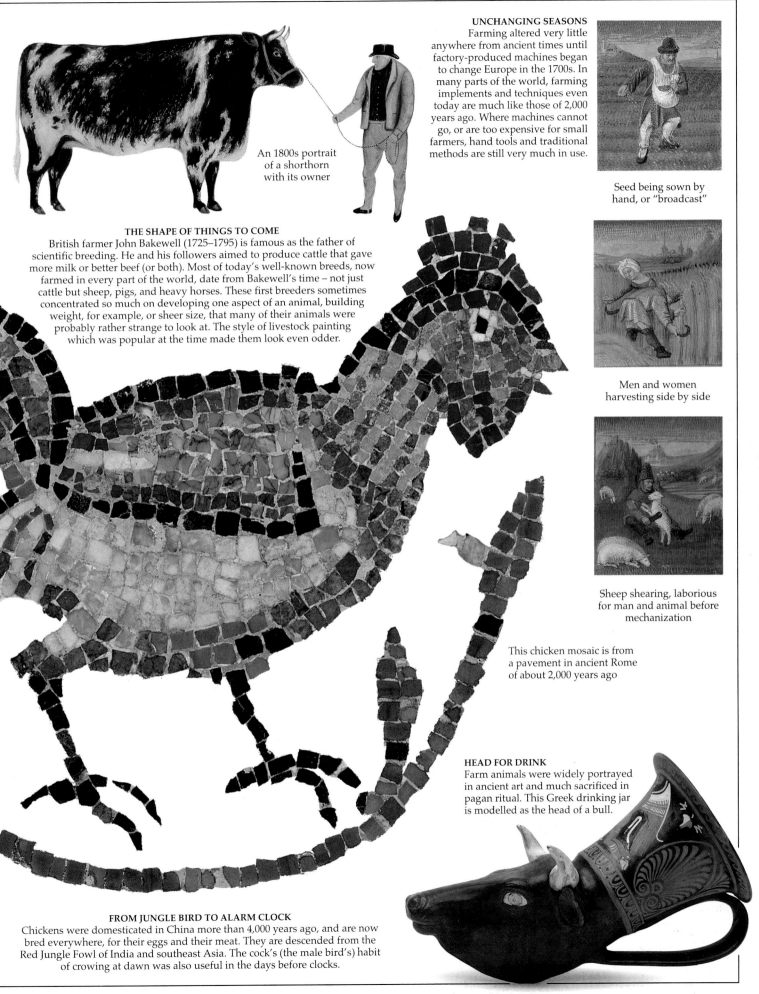

An 1800s portrait
of a shorthorn
with its owner

UNCHANGING SEASONS
Farming altered very little anywhere from ancient times until factory-produced machines began to change Europe in the 1700s. In many parts of the world, farming implements and techniques even today are much like those of 2,000 years ago. Where machines cannot go, or are too expensive for small farmers, hand tools and traditional methods are still very much in use.

Seed being sown by
hand, or "broadcast"

THE SHAPE OF THINGS TO COME
British farmer John Bakewell (1725–1795) is famous as the father of scientific breeding. He and his followers aimed to produce cattle that gave more milk or better beef (or both). Most of today's well-known breeds, now farmed in every part of the world, date from Bakewell's time – not just cattle but sheep, pigs, and heavy horses. These first breeders sometimes concentrated so much on developing one aspect of an animal, building weight, for example, or sheer size, that many of their animals were probably rather strange to look at. The style of livestock painting which was popular at the time made them look even odder.

Men and women
harvesting side by side

Sheep shearing, laborious
for man and animal before
mechanization

This chicken mosaic is from
a pavement in ancient Rome
of about 2,000 years ago

HEAD FOR DRINK
Farm animals were widely portrayed in ancient art and much sacrificed in pagan ritual. This Greek drinking jar is modelled as the head of a bull.

FROM JUNGLE BIRD TO ALARM CLOCK
Chickens were domesticated in China more than 4,000 years ago, and are now bred everywhere, for their eggs and their meat. They are descended from the Red Jungle Fowl of India and southeast Asia. The cock's (the male bird's) habit of crowing at dawn was also useful in the days before clocks.

Animal power

PEOPLE FIRST BEGAN to tame and breed cattle and horses thousands of years ago in the Stone Age. Later, about 3500 B.C., ox-drawn ploughs created the original fields. The first wheeled carts, pulled by oxen or horses, meant farmers could move much greater loads – and trade their produce on a commercial basis. Oxen were the first true beasts of burden – any kind of cattle used for draught (pulling) work are called oxen. Strong but docile, they also provided milk, and meat and skin at the end of their working lives. Heavy horses began to replace them in Europe in the 18th century, because they could pull new farm equipment such as all-iron ploughs, seed drills, and harrows very much faster. In their turn, early this century, horses were outdone for speed and strength by the tractor. In poorer countries animal power still pulls the plough.

A DONKEY'S LIFE
In many countries animals are still working just as they have for thousands of years. Donkeys, descended from the wild asses of Africa and Asia, have served farmers since the days of ancient Greece. Even today, in Greece alone, 250,000 of these humble beasts of burden labour patiently, bearing heavy loads. This donkey is at work on the island of Corfu.

ONE HORSE POWER
Two-wheeled carts such as this "tumbril" could carry half a tonne of crops such as turnips, potatoes, hay, or corn, or of farmyard manure to spread on the fields. The load could be piled high with extensions called "harvest ladders" fitted at each end. Big four-wheeled wagons could take loads of four tonnes.

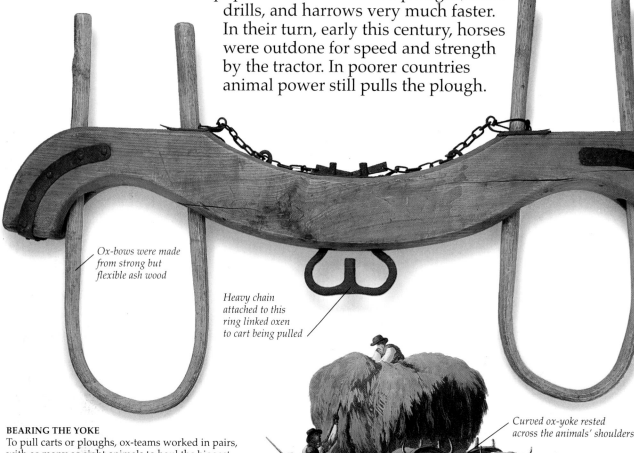

Ox-bows were made from strong but flexible ash wood

Heavy chain attached to this ring linked oxen to cart being pulled

Curved ox-yoke rested across the animals' shoulders

BEARING THE YOKE
To pull carts or ploughs, ox-teams worked in pairs, with as many as eight animals to haul the biggest loads. Oxen were harnessed with an ox-yoke, a chunky one-piece wooden beam. Ox-bows were then passed round each ox's neck and through holes drilled into the yoke. Locked in position, these spread the load and stopped the ox escaping. From the 1700s, as horses came into use more and more on farms, European cattle breeders tried to produce oxen with greater pulling power, but none could match the heavy horse, and draught oxen gradually became a rare sight in Europe.

Harnessed into fixed collars, the horses stayed where they were, and the treadmill revolved, turning the drum of the threshing machine

MADE FOR WALKING
Horse power found new uses with the arrival of agricultural machinery. This Belgian threshing machine of about 1875 was operated by a treadmill – a revolving walkway, like a big conveyor belt, which the horses turned simply by walking on it.

Blinkers prevent distraction

Horse collar, made to measure in padded leather, helps to distribute the load to the animal's chest and shoulders without cutting into the windpipe

HARNESSED STRENGTH
Farm horses are trained gradually. First they learn to pull implements such as the harrow and plough. Pulling carts comes later. Fully grown at six to seven years, draught horses can live more than 20 years, as long a life as a tractor. Unlike tractors, they need only hay and grass for fuel (plus a few supplements, such as root vegetables, and calcium to help bones develop).

The tractor

LATE LAST CENTURY, the first tractors were built. They were useful for planting, cultivating, harvesting, and countless other tasks around the farm. By the 1920s modern-style all-purpose tractors had been developed. Wherever farmers could afford them, they were soon very popular. Within a generation, in many countries, they had put the farm horse into history books. The tractors of today are even more versatile, and they are awesomely powerful. As well as pulling loads that would bring 100 horses to a standstill, they can drive all kinds of mechanized attachments, from mowing machines to earth-moving equipment.

THE DAYS OF STEAM
Steam engines were first used in farming more than 200 years ago, long before tractors were invented. Their usefulness was limited because they were enormously heavy and guzzled tonnes of coal and water. Steam power was mainly used on farms in the form of traction engines hauling ploughs and other equipment from field to field. Fowler's Ploughing Engine (above) was used from the 1860s onwards (pp. 12–13). It was part of a system in which two steam engines, at opposite sides of a field, drove a plough that cut six furrows at a time. Unlike a modern tractor it was too heavy to drive onto the field itself. When tractors were developed, steam engines were soon forgotten.

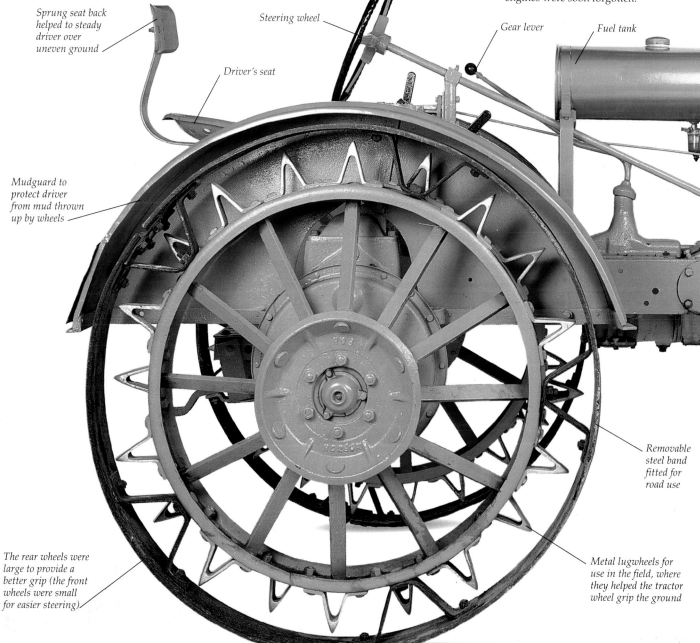

Sprung seat back helped to steady driver over uneven ground

Steering wheel

Gear lever

Fuel tank

Driver's seat

Mudguard to protect driver from mud thrown up by wheels

Removable steel band fitted for road use

The rear wheels were large to provide a better grip (the front wheels were small for easier steering)

Metal lugwheels for use in the field, where they helped the tractor wheel grip the ground

A FORD FOR FARMS
The Fordson was one of the first mass-produced tractors. It was produced by US car manufacturer Ford from 1916 onwards, and sold worldwide. The Fordson had a ploughing speed of 4.5 km/h (2.8 mph), and weighed just over a tonne. It ran on paraffin, which was then cheaper than petrol, but today's diesel engines are far more efficient. Tractors like this could plough 3 hectares (8 acres) on one tank of fuel.

POWER LIFTERS
Tractors can do things undreamed of in the era of horsepower, such as lifting these giant bales of silage (pp. 34–35). Hydraulic equipment means farmers can pick up and transport items weighing a tonne or more.

Tractors are able to lift and pull heavy objects using hydraulic power systems, which transfer power in a very flexible way

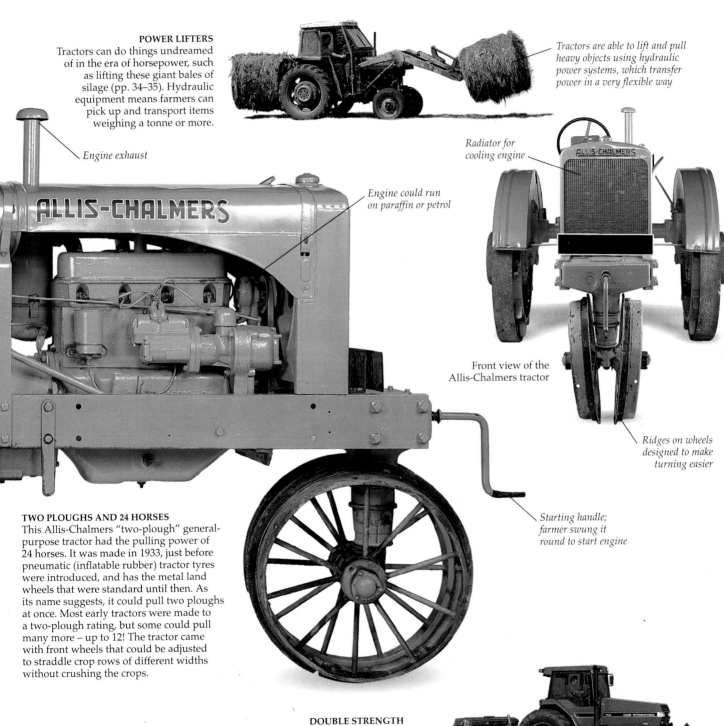

Engine exhaust

Engine could run on paraffin or petrol

Radiator for cooling engine

Front view of the Allis-Chalmers tractor

Ridges on wheels designed to make turning easier

Starting handle; farmer swung it round to start engine

TWO PLOUGHS AND 24 HORSES
This Allis-Chalmers "two-plough" general-purpose tractor had the pulling power of 24 horses. It was made in 1933, just before pneumatic (inflatable rubber) tractor tyres were introduced, and has the metal land wheels that were standard until then. As its name suggests, it could pull two ploughs at once. Most early tractors were made to a two-plough rating, but some could pull many more – up to 12! The tractor came with front wheels that could be adjusted to straddle crop rows of different widths without crushing the crops.

DOUBLE STRENGTH
Modern tractors have so much power that they can operate ploughs and other machinery at both ends. The machines are often mounted on the tractor and are hydraulically operated.

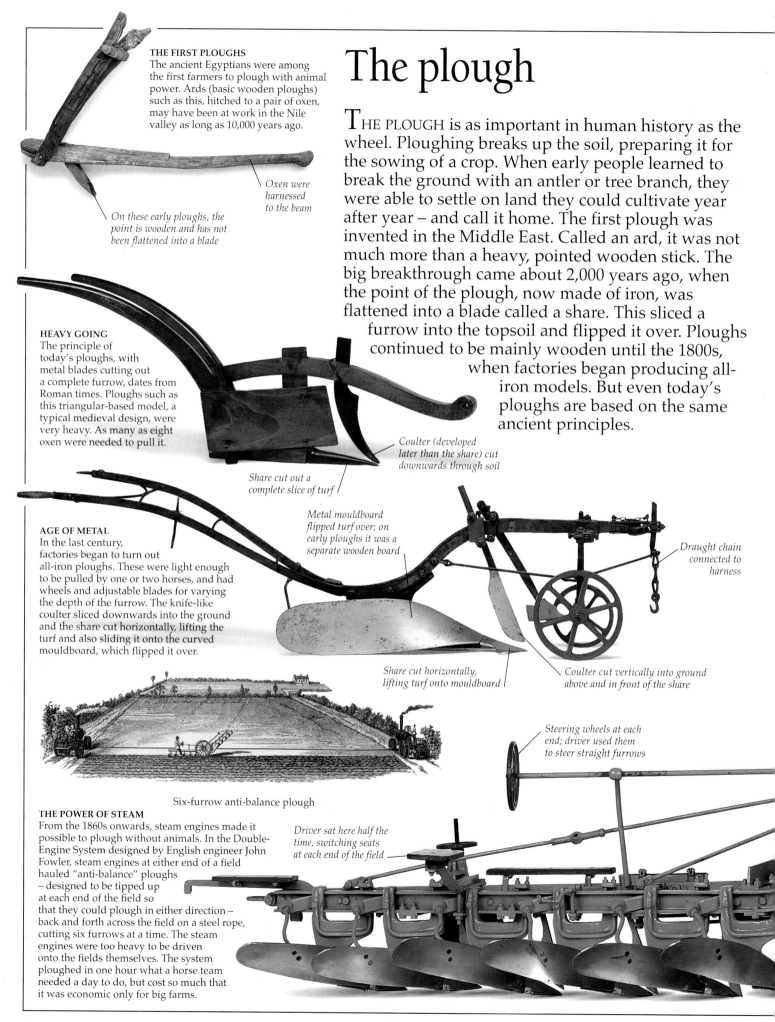

THE FIRST PLOUGHS
The ancient Egyptians were among the first farmers to plough with animal power. Ards (basic wooden ploughs) such as this, hitched to a pair of oxen, may have been at work in the Nile valley as long as 10,000 years ago.

Oxen were harnessed to the beam

On these early ploughs, the point is wooden and has not been flattened into a blade

The plough

THE PLOUGH is as important in human history as the wheel. Ploughing breaks up the soil, preparing it for the sowing of a crop. When early people learned to break the ground with an antler or tree branch, they were able to settle on land they could cultivate year after year – and call it home. The first plough was invented in the Middle East. Called an ard, it was not much more than a heavy, pointed wooden stick. The big breakthrough came about 2,000 years ago, when the point of the plough, now made of iron, was flattened into a blade called a share. This sliced a furrow into the topsoil and flipped it over. Ploughs continued to be mainly wooden until the 1800s, when factories began producing all-iron models. But even today's ploughs are based on the same ancient principles.

HEAVY GOING
The principle of today's ploughs, with metal blades cutting out a complete furrow, dates from Roman times. Ploughs such as this triangular-based model, a typical medieval design, were very heavy. As many as eight oxen were needed to pull it.

Coulter (developed later than the share) cut downwards through soil

Share cut out a complete slice of turf

Metal mouldboard flipped turf over; on early ploughs it was a separate wooden board

Draught chain connected to harness

AGE OF METAL
In the last century, factories began to turn out all-iron ploughs. These were light enough to be pulled by one or two horses, and had wheels and adjustable blades for varying the depth of the furrow. The knife-like coulter sliced downwards into the ground and the share cut horizontally, lifting the turf and also sliding it onto the curved mouldboard, which flipped it over.

Share cut horizontally, lifting turf onto mouldboard

Coulter cut vertically into ground above and in front of the share

Steering wheels at each end; driver used them to steer straight furrows

Six-furrow anti-balance plough

THE POWER OF STEAM
From the 1860s onwards, steam engines made it possible to plough without animals. In the Double-Engine System designed by English engineer John Fowler, steam engines at either end of a field hauled "anti-balance" ploughs – designed to be tipped up at each end of the field so that they could plough in either direction – back and forth across the field on a steel rope, cutting six furrows at a time. The steam engines were too heavy to be driven onto the fields themselves. The system ploughed in one hour what a horse team needed a day to do, but cost so much that it was economic only for big farms.

Driver sat here half the time, switching seats at each end of the field

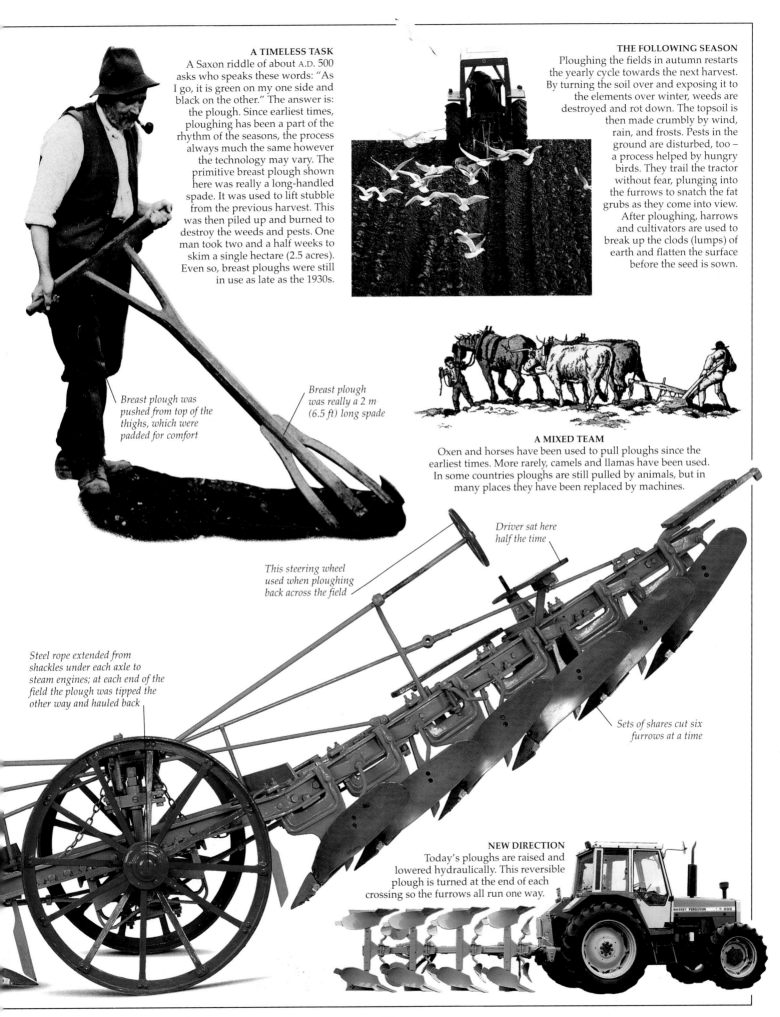

A TIMELESS TASK
A Saxon riddle of about A.D. 500 asks who speaks these words: "As I go, it is green on my one side and black on the other." The answer is: the plough. Since earliest times, ploughing has been a part of the rhythm of the seasons, the process always much the same however the technology may vary. The primitive breast plough shown here was really a long-handled spade. It was used to lift stubble from the previous harvest. This was then piled up and burned to destroy the weeds and pests. One man took two and a half weeks to skim a single hectare (2.5 acres). Even so, breast ploughs were still in use as late as the 1930s.

Breast plough was pushed from top of the thighs, which were padded for comfort

Breast plough was really a 2 m (6.5 ft) long spade

THE FOLLOWING SEASON
Ploughing the fields in autumn restarts the yearly cycle towards the next harvest. By turning the soil over and exposing it to the elements over winter, weeds are destroyed and rot down. The topsoil is then made crumbly by wind, rain, and frosts. Pests in the ground are disturbed, too – a process helped by hungry birds. They trail the tractor without fear, plunging into the furrows to snatch the fat grubs as they come into view. After ploughing, harrows and cultivators are used to break up the clods (lumps) of earth and flatten the surface before the seed is sown.

A MIXED TEAM
Oxen and horses have been used to pull ploughs since the earliest times. More rarely, camels and llamas have been used. In some countries ploughs are still pulled by animals, but in many places they have been replaced by machines.

This steering wheel used when ploughing back across the field

Driver sat here half the time

Steel rope extended from shackles under each axle to steam engines; at each end of the field the plough was tipped the other way and hauled back

Sets of shares cut six furrows at a time

NEW DIRECTION
Today's ploughs are raised and lowered hydraulically. This reversible plough is turned at the end of each crossing so the furrows all run one way.

Fields and soil

THE FIRST FIELDS WERE SQUARE because Stone Age farmers had to plough the soil twice, cross-wise, to make it ready for sowing. When furrow-turning ploughs were invented, this was no longer necessary and fields became longer. For centuries, arable land (land on which crops are grown) was largely made up of long strips, farmed by families to feed themselves. Change began in Europe, with the Industrial Revolution of the 1700s. Towns started to grow. Demand for food increased. Strips were absorbed into large fields, in which new equipment could be used efficiently. Crops were rotated to keep the soil fertile and to produce fodder harvests for the booming business of livestock farming for meat production. Industrial-scale farming had begun.

Rapeseed

Grass and clover

A four-crop pattern of rotation, with grazing

Wheat

Wheat

Turnips

Horses pulled the all-iron rollers of the 1800s

ROTATE FOR RESULTS
For centuries crop rotation has enabled farmers to make use of the same fields year after year without exhausting the soil. A field which grew wheat one year could be planted with turnips or rapeseed the next. Such crops provide animal feed in winter, and hopefully clear the soil of diseases that might attack future cereal crops. (Rapeseed also makes vegetable oil.) Grass and clover were also planted in some years, providing grazing for livestock, which enriched the soil with their manure.

JUST KEEPS ROLLING ALONG
After the plough comes the roller to break down the biggest clods of earth and provide a level surface for sowing. The first rollers were so heavy that it took teams of oxen to drag them along.

The implement was connected by chain to the horse harness

CRUSHING PROGRESS
Before ox- and horse-drawn rollers first came into use in the late Middle Ages, ploughed land was broken down very laboriously with mallet-like hand tools called beetles. The first rollers were simply tree trunks or cylindrical stones. Iron rollers produced in factories gradually took their place from about 1800 onwards. This Kit Kat Roll of the mid 1800s consisted of a strong frame with spars to level the surface, holding a roller shaped like an elongated barrel with heavy metal bands encircling its middle. The effect was to crush the clods where it mattered most – in the furrow – while the roller's ends bore down evenly on either side.

EARLY TECHNOLOGY
Harrows were invented because farmers needed to break up and loosen the topsoil before sowing the seed. Early harrows consisted of tough bushes such as gorse or hawthorn attached to logs or wooden frames.

Shape of roller concentrated its weight into the furrow made earlier by the plough, along which the draught horse walked

SPRING ACTION
The cultivator is a development of the harrow. It breaks up the ploughed surface with rows of spring-mounted tines (pointed prongs) attached to a heavy steel frame towed behind a tractor.

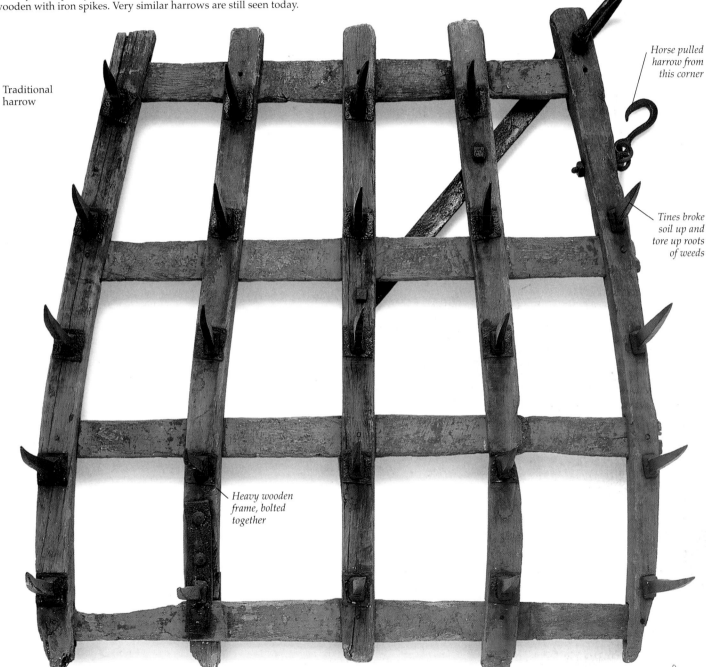

Traditional harrow

Horse pulled harrow from this corner

Tines broke soil up and tore up roots of weeds

Heavy wooden frame, bolted together

HARROWING EXPERIENCE
Tilth is the name given to soil that is fine and crumbly, and thus ready for sowing. The harrow, hauled over the ploughed and rolled ground, is the implement that produces the tilth. Early harrows consisted of sturdy timbers bolted together to form a square frame, bearing iron spikes called tines. They were pulled, spikes-down, by oxen or horses. Like rollers, harrows became more sophisticated from about 1800. All-iron diamond-shaped and triangular models made lighter work of the job. Today's steel harrows can be mounted behind tractors and hydraulically raised and lowered. Special versions include the disc harrow, which breaks down ploughed furrows by slicing through them with rows of circular blades.

Before seed drills, harrows were used like rakes to cover up the seed in the newly planted soil

Sowing the seed

ONCE THE SOIL HAS BEEN PREPARED, sowing begins. In the days before machines, seed was scattered by hand on the fields. But much of it was lost, because it fell on the surface among wild seeds whose shoots could later choke the crop, and birds ate it before it could be covered up. The answer came about 1700 when English farmer Jethro Tull invented the seed drill. This was a machine that cut several parallel grooves in the soil, and then dropped the seed in neat rows called drills. As the crop grew, the farmer kept the weeds down using a horse-drawn hoeing machine with blades spaced to fit between rows. Today's tractor-drawn sowing machinery is just a refined version of Tull's inspired invention.

AN EARLY FORM OF BROADCASTING
The ancient method of scattering the seed over the open ground was called broadcasting, because it scattered seed everywhere. It was a wasteful method of sowing. Farmers knew that only a fraction of the seed would successfully sprout – just as the old proverb says: "One for the pigeon; one for the crow; one to wither and one to grow". Here the sower in a 15th-century French scene is accompanied not just by the pigeons and crows, but by a serious-faced assistant trying to net the hungry birds – perhaps hoping to put them into a pie as well as saving the crop.

Lever engaged drive chain to cog wheel, which it then turned

Cog wheel rotated brush inside hopper, which swept seeds down the tube

Seeds were held in hopper

SOWING BACKWARDS
The seed drill was not the only method of sowing designed to minimise waste. Dibbling – making two rows of holes for individual seeds with a pair of pointed sticks – ensured the seeds were at the right depth, and spaced evenly. The dibbler walked backwards to avoid treading on the holes as he went. It was labour-intensive, but an important means of sowing in the 18th century, providing valuable work for country people at a time when there were few jobs in the countryside.

THIS IS NOT A WHEELBARROW
Most seed drills were horse-drawn, but this small 19th-century seed drill was pushed by a man instead. As he pushed it along, the big wheels powered a chain. The chain turned a cog wheel. The cog wheel rotated a brush inside the hopper. The brush swept an even flow of seeds down the tube into the 25 mm (1 in) deep furrow cut by the blade in front of the tube.

FODDER TURNIP SEED
Standard turnips for animal food are planted in early summer and fast-growing ones in late summer – all for autumn harvesting.

WHITE CLOVER SEED
Bred from wild clover, it is often mixed with grass seed to provide pasture for cattle and sheep, and nectar for bees.

HYBRID RYE-GRASS SEED
Once planted, rye-grass reseeds itself for many years to provide lasting grassland. It makes good grazing, hay, and silage.

WHEAT SEED
Wheat can be sown in autumn or spring. "Winter wheat" grows more slowly than "spring wheat" but produces a heavier crop.

QUAINT BUT EFFECTIVE

Even the earliest seed drills increased farmers' productivity considerably. The 19th century saw further development, leading to machines such as this eight-row self-adjusting model of 1871. Modern tractor-drawn sowing machines are another huge step forward.

Jethro Tull (1674–1741) trained as a lawyer but chose to live at his father's farm

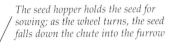

The seed hopper holds the seed for sowing; as the wheel turns, the seed falls down the chute into the furrow

NOT TOTALLY NEW

Seed drills such as this one seemed revolutionary in Britain in the 1700s, but they were not the first the world had ever seen. Types of seed drills were used by the Romans, and the ancient Chinese had a version of their own in 2800 B.C.

CREATOR OF THE SEED DRILL

English inventor Jethro Tull was the organist in his local church, and the instrument's pipes gave him the idea for the "corn drill" he invented in 1700. By feeding the seeds down tubes into the furrows it cut into the soil, the horse-drawn machine produced straight rows. These could be weeded with a horse-drawn hoe or plough as the crop grew. After much research, Tull finally made his system public in 1731 in one of the most important farming books ever written. It had the catchy title *Horsehoeing Husbandry*.

Unusual iron tyre, bolted on to the spokes of the wheel

HE'S GOT RHYTHM

Hand sowers often carried the seed in a seed-lip. It was a wooden or iron container shaped to fit against the body, supported by a strap across the shoulder. The sower moved with measured steps, scattering the grain in a constant rhythm to left and right for an even spread over the soil.

Large wheel drove chain and made drill light to manoeuvre

Protecting the crop

From the sowing of the seed to the final harvest, crops are at nature's mercy. Today, science helps farmers to fight off their four main enemies: wildlife, insects, weeds, and diseases. Rabbits, once a serious threat to sprouting crops, have been controlled by methods including the deliberate introduction of the disease myxomatosis. Birds are frightened off by less deadly means – such as scarers emitting loud, shotgun-like bangs. Chemical sprays are used against less visible threats, although these substances are very expensive and are controlled by tough government rules, so farmers use them as sparingly as possible. Before these methods became available, farmers tried all sorts of fascinating means of fending off nature's attacks. And many of the old methods still have their uses even in today's technological age.

BIRD ON A WIRE
Realistic-looking models of predators have long been, and still are, suspended from poles or trees in the fields by farmers hoping to keep birds away from their crops. But even scarers such as this colourful hawk will only fool the most bird-brained seed-stealer for a limited time.

Rattle was swung around to make a noise

JOB FOR THE BOY
Before modern, automated bird-scaring, the task of shooing away hungry raiders with clappers, a rattle, or other noisemakers, was given to children. Out in all weathers, it was often miserable work, and lonely, too. Farmers would send just one child, knowing that two or more would only distract each other. As one old saying had it, "One boy is a boy. Two boys is half a boy. Three boys is no boy at all."

MADE TO SCARE
Scarecrows are simple to make. You just need two 2 m (6.5 ft) poles tied as a cross and draped with an old coat and pair of trousers, perhaps also stuffed with straw. They are an economical means of trying to frighten off birds. The effect is traditionally boosted by making a head from a large turnip, carving out the facial features, and crowning the masterpiece with a suitable hat.

Clappers consisted of a wooden bat with an extra piece tied either side and were waved vigorously at the approach of marauding birds

BAD NEWS FOR CABBAGES
"Cabbage whites" are among the few butterflies that can be described as pests to farmers. The large white and small white species lay their eggs – two broods a year – on many kinds of wild plant, including cabbages. The caterpillars can do serious damage to the crop, which may have to be sprayed with an insecticide.

Growing crops provide birds and other pests with many meals, but farmers do their best to spoil the feast

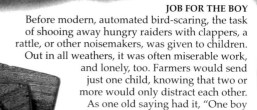

Aerial crop sprays must be used in dry, windless conditions; if they land away from the crops they are intended for they can have very harmful effects on animals, plants, and people

Articulated wings flapping in the breeze add to the deterrent effect

SPRAY TIME
Crops are sprayed for a lot of different reasons. "Selective" weedkillers destroy particularly harmful weeds without damaging the crop itself, as do sprays that target certain insects, such as aphids (greenfly), or serious diseases such as potato blight. Sprayers are most commonly pulled by tractor, but on very large farms it can be more economical to spray from an aircraft.

Bright colouring makes the hawk more visible and more frightening

DARKENING THE SKY
Swarms of locusts such as this one in Ethiopia devour all vegetation on which they land. Such swarms can cover an area bigger than a town, but locusts can usually be kept down by spraying from aircraft.

MOTH TO THE RESCUE
Friend or foe? Few butterfly or moth species are pests, and some are quite the opposite. This is the cinnabar moth, whose larvae eat the weed ragwort.

WELL TRAVELLED WEED
Thistle seed, spread by the wind, can germinate over a long period. "One year's weeds; seven years' seeds", is the country saying.

UPLIFT FOR DOCKS
Docks are among many weeds with deep roots which, if merely cut off at ground level before the crop is sown, will regrow and choke the young shoots. Among several tools designed in the past for extracting the whole root of docks and thistles is this dock lifter.

Harvesting by hand

FROM EARLIEST TIMES until the 19th century, grain and hay were cut entirely by sickle and scythe. With the sharpest steel blade a reaper of 150 years ago could cut about 0.1 hectares (0.3 acres) in a day. In the late-summer heat, it was exhausting work, made urgent by the need to keep the harvest dry. Rain could ruin the crop, so the reapers were closely followed by the sheaf-makers, who tied the corn into sheaves (bunches), collected the sheaves, and stood them together in "stooks" to dry in the sun. Once ready, or as soon as the weather threatened to turn, the sheaves were carted to ricks (large stacks) or the barn to await threshing. Finally the gleaners collected left-over corn. For hay-making in early summer, grass was cut by the same methods and allowed to dry in the open before being stored as winter fodder (animal feed).

LONG DAYS IN THE SUN
Harvesting brought hard but welcome work for most of the rural population, gathering in the crop throughout the daylight hours. Since the coming of the machine, far fewer people have been needed, either for harvesting or for farming generally.

The toothed sickle sawed the wheat, while the stalks were held with the other hand

THE OLDEST BLADE
Toothed sickles are the oldest harvesting tools, starting as curved flint blades in the Stone Age. The sickle used by this French reaper of c. 1200 was probably made of iron.

The long handle, called a sned, could be either bent or straight

Cradle makes it easier to gather cut stalks

Crook to hold stalks together as they were cut

Hook has broad, sharp blade

The blade, of iron or steel, was 60 cm– 1.20 m (2–4 ft) long

GRIM REAPERS
Grain and hay have been harvested by scythe since Roman times. The long handle of the hay scythe allowed the mower to work at a comfortable stoop, swinging the blade just above the ground. Scythes usually had two main grips, and some had an attachment to gather the cut stalks.

STEEL IS SMOOTHER
In the 19th century, the toothed iron sickle began to give way to the smooth-edged steel sickle, also called the scythe hook. These were heavier than earlier harvesting tools, with broad, sharp blades which enabled the reaper to shear through the stalks in one motion. Some were used with a crook, which held the stalks together for the cut.

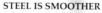

Sturdy wooden teeth to rake in loose fragments

Barley fork had three tines

Common fork had two tines

LEFTOVERS
After the harvest, gleanings could be gathered in by the farm labourers' families, or by the poor of the parish, to provide a useful extra source of grain in times when food was short.

WHAT A DRAG
A wooden drag rake that could be up to 2 m (6.5 ft) wide was pulled by hand over the stubble to collect up quantities of loose corn or hay stalks missed by the sheaf-makers.

Common pitchfork for hay and corn

The common fork was up to 2 m (6.5 ft) long, the barley fork even longer; the handles were made of wood

Pitchfork for barley, made from a single piece of wood

HARVESTER'S MEAL BASKET
Farm workers' meals were simple. In a country such as Britain, the main meal would include bread, perhaps some smoked meat and raw onions, and cold tea (without milk or sugar) carried in an old bottle.

PILE IT HIGH
Corn and hay were piled high onto carts for transport and stacking back at the farm. Long-handled forks enabled the labourers to pitch the sheaves high onto the top of the laden cart or stack.

TINE TALE
Using a pitchfork took skill and strength. The common fork, with two metal tines (prongs), was used to lift hay and corn. The barley fork, with three tines, was even longer, because cut barley is lighter and more can be lifted at a time, provided it is well supported on the fork.

Skilled labourers could lift great weights of hay or corn with their pitchforks

Threshing and winnowing

THWACK! THWACK! THWACK! The sound of threshing rang through winter for thousands of years – long before the clatter of horses' hooves or the din of machinery ever disturbed the countryside. At harvest time the corn had been left to dry out in stacks. Now it was threshed (beaten). The threshers hit it with jointed wooden tools called flails to knock the grain off the stalks. Once the grain had been collected up it was tossed in the air (winnowed) to get rid of chaff (straw dust). The light chaff blew away, the heavier grain fell back to the floor. The straw (the stalks of the corn) might be used for feed, roofing, hats, or baskets. The grain was sold, or used for seed or for feed.

Grain

Stalks

STANDS ON STADDLES
Large stacks of corn, called ricks, were built on stack stands. Stands – such as the cast iron example on the right – rested on mushroom-shaped legs called staddles.

BEATING FOR A PURPOSE
Men threshed in pairs, working rhythmically to keep up their pace and avoid painful clashes. It was warm work, and skilled – clumsy use of the flail could mean a broken skull.

ALL TIED UP
Sheaves of wheat or barley were stored upright to dry out for a few days, then collected and stacked. The sheaves were traditionally bound with straw rope, but when mechanical harvesting began in the mid 1800s (pp. 26–27), string was used.

CLASSIC DESIGN
The basic design of the flail is ancient, dating back into prehistory, but flails did vary a little according to local conditions. The handle, about a metre long, was longer than the beating rod, and was connected to it by a thong called a swipple (or swingle), made of eelskin or leather.

Traditional flail

Beating rod of blackthorn or hardwood

Handle of ash

WIND AND THE WINNOWERS
Inside an open barn the winnowers had a through draught to carry away the chaff as they tossed the grain from their baskets and shovels. The grain, retained within the barn by "thresholds" at the doors, was collected up and bagged for storage or sale.

Yoke for carrying straw

AIRING THE PARTICLES
Chaff riddles like this one and shallow baskets called winnowing fans were used both to sieve out smaller particles and to toss the grain, so the dust would blow away in the air. Wider-mesh sieves separated grains of differing size, as well as unthreshed ears and straw.

Frames usually made of steamed oak or ash

Rake-like "comb"

KINGSIZE COMB
To protect the harvest from rain, stacks were thatched with straw from the first threshings. Thatchers carried bundles of straw up ladders on a yoke and positioned them securely in overlapping rows. The thatcher used a large, rake-like "comb" to rake out weeds and short straws.

STACKS AND STACKS
Until combine harvesters began to be used, 50 years or so ago, the crop always had to be stored to await threshing. Sheaves were built into large stacks with sloping tops. The stacks were then thatched for weatherproofing, because damp could make the grain sprout and become useless. Shapes varied, but round ones up to 6 m (20 ft) wide and high were common.

Threshing by machine

A NEW SOUND RANG OUT from the farmyards and fields when the engines of the steam age began to take over the task of separating the grain from the straw. It had all begun in 1786 when a Scotsman, Andrew Meikle, invented a machine that threshed corn by rubbing it between rollers, not by whacking it in the traditional way. Later machines also included the process of winnowing, by blowing away chaff with rotating fans. For a short time, these new machines were powered by horse teams, but steam engines soon took over. This ended a major source of winter work for farm labourers, and there were riots. But nothing could stand in the way of the machine. Today, progress has brought us the combine harvester, and traditional threshing and winnowing have become part of farming history.

LAST DAYS FOR SHEAVES
Wheat sheaves were bound and stacked for machine threshing just as they had been in the days of the hand flail. Sheaves and cornstacks only disappeared from the fields with the arrival of the combine harvester in the 20th century.

MACHINERY ON THE MOVE
From the 1850s, steam engines began to appear on farms, first in Britain and then in other countries. This equipment was operated by contractors, whose arrival each year became something of an event. The machines were driven up to the cornstacks and connected up. Then work began. While one man with a flail could thresh a quarter of a tonne of wheat in a day, and a horse-driven machine up to seven tonnes, a steam-powered thresher produced as many as 25 tonnes. But several men were still needed: a driver to stoke the engine with coal and keep it supplied with water, men to fork and feed in the sheaves, another to change the sacks as they filled, others to collect and bale the straw.

Straw travels up elevator and is tipped off onto stack

Corn is fed in here; inside, a drum separates grain from straw; grain and chaff fall through a series of screens to the bottom of the machine

Straw exits here, passing from the straw shaker onto an elevator

Wheels made the machine fully mobile

Chaff separated from the grain by fans falls out here

Grain collects here and is carried up by this elevator

Sacks are attached here to collect grain carried up by the elevator

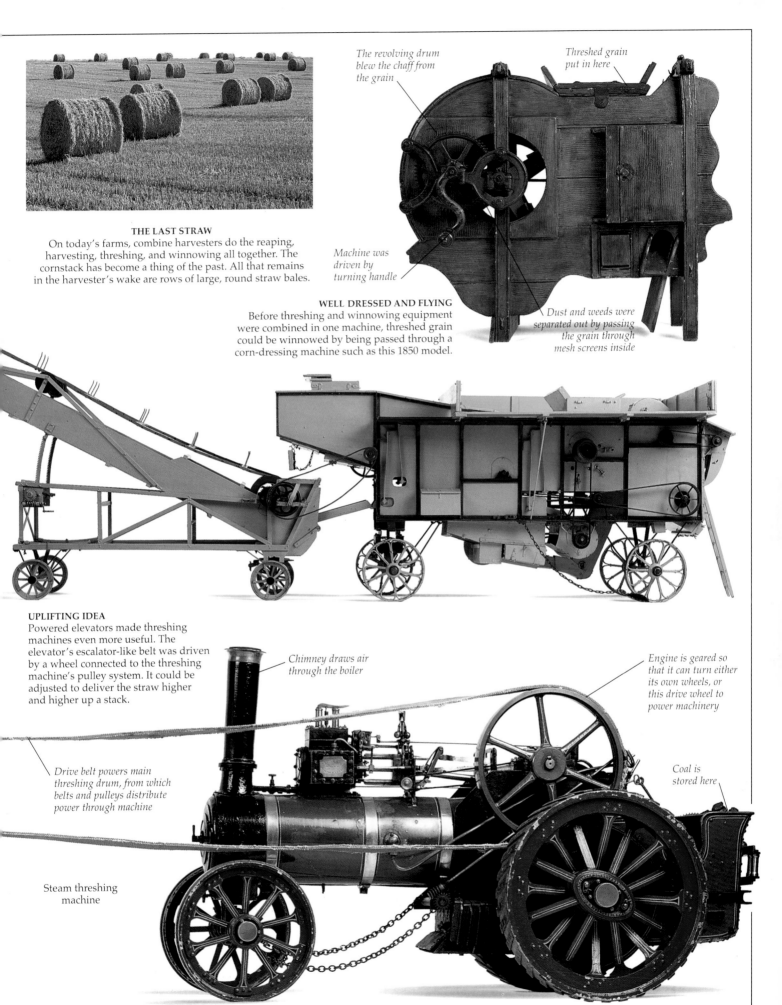

THE LAST STRAW
On today's farms, combine harvesters do the reaping, harvesting, threshing, and winnowing all together. The cornstack has become a thing of the past. All that remains in the harvester's wake are rows of large, round straw bales.

The revolving drum blew the chaff from the grain

Threshed grain put in here

Machine was driven by turning handle

Dust and weeds were separated out by passing the grain through mesh screens inside

WELL DRESSED AND FLYING
Before threshing and winnowing equipment were combined in one machine, threshed grain could be winnowed by being passed through a corn-dressing machine such as this 1850 model.

UPLIFTING IDEA
Powered elevators made threshing machines even more useful. The elevator's escalator-like belt was driven by a wheel connected to the threshing machine's pulley system. It could be adjusted to deliver the straw higher and higher up a stack.

Chimney draws air through the boiler

Engine is geared so that it can turn either its own wheels, or this drive wheel to power machinery

Drive belt powers main threshing drum, from which belts and pulleys distribute power through machine

Coal is stored here

Steam threshing machine

Harvesting by machine

LEAVING HOME
The tiny harvest mouse is often seen at harvest time, when it has to abandon its cornfield home as the reapers approach.

LITTLE MORE than a century ago, when most harvesting was still carried out by hand, it was a long day's work for more than a dozen farmworkers to cut two hectares (five acres) of barley or wheat and bind it into sheaves. More work lay ahead to stack the crop and later extract the grain by threshing it. Today, a combine harvester with one driver turns two hectares of wheat into grain in under an hour. This miracle of mechanization began when the first successful reaping machine was invented by an American farmer, Cyrus McCormick, in about 1840. It worked rather like a huge pair of scissors. Pulled through the corn by horses, it had a revolving reel which pressed the stalks against a fixed blade and sheared them off. The principle behind mechanical harvesters has remained the same ever since, with many ingenious refinements along the way.

SAILING THE FIELDS
The horse-drawn "sail reaper" appeared in 1862, just before the reaper-binder. It could harvest two hectares (five acres) a day. The rake-like arms lifted swathes of cut corn and laid them behind the machine to be bound into sheaves.

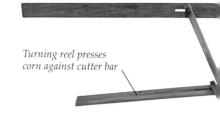

Turning reel presses corn against cutter bar

BOUND TO DO WELL
This 1930s reaper-binder was state-of-the-art technology in its time. It cut the crop with a rotating reel which pressed the corn against the fixed cutting bar. Elaborate gears linked the wheels to the reel, the moving canvas platform, and the elevator, using the motion of the wheels to power the rest. The stalks were tied into sheaves in the binding mechanism, and then dropped to the ground for collection.

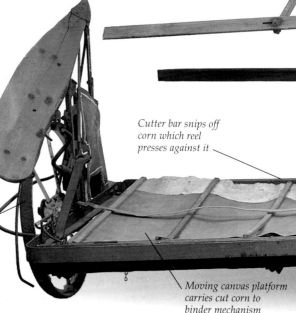

Cutter bar snips off corn which reel presses against it

Land wheels used in fields

Moving canvas platform carries cut corn to binder mechanism

PICTURES OF PROGRESS
First introduced on American prairie farms, reaper-binders dominated harvesting from the late 1800s until early this century. They were the first machines to combine the tasks of cutting the crop and binding it into sheaves. Early models were pulled by horses, later versions by tractors. Reaper-binders were operated by one driver, plus two or three workers to collect the sheaves and set them up to dry. This way, three or four people could harvest 0.4 hectares (one acre) an hour – ten times what the same team could have done before mechanization.

THE HOT SEAT
Early reaper-binders were not the most pleasant machines to drive. This illustration of 1878 shows how the driver had to sit between the reel and the binding mechanism, both spinning fiercely.

SPEED IN THE FIELD
Modern combine harvesters work so fast that they can reap the crop while all the grain is at its best, and before dry weather has a chance to change to rain. They can also harvest "laid crops", cereals flattened by rain and wind, which the old reaping machines could not have salvaged.

Grain emptied from here at intervals into tractor-drawn trailers

Straw ejected here

MIGHTY MACHINES
Today's harvesting machines are called combine harvesters because they combine the functions of cutting, collecting, threshing, and winnowing the crop. One harvester does work that would have occupied dozens of farm labourers even in the days of reaper-binders, cutting great swathes through the corn. The huge reel in front may be 5m (16ft) or more wide. The grain is extracted, sieved, stored briefly, then poured into a trailer.

Elevator works like an escalator, delivering cut corn into the binding mechanism

Packer arms hold sheaf until bound, then release it

Driver sits here to steer and control the machine

Gear wheels transfer power from wheels to binder, elevator, and moving canvas platform

This land wheel is raised while road wheels in use; road wheels are removed for work in fields

Road wheels are used when the reaper-binder is being towed between fields; they face sideways because it is easier to tow the machine that way round

A hare startled by the harvesters

Wheat to bread

THE FIRST BREAD was made in the Nile valley, more than 10,000 years ago. It was there that hunter-gatherers discovered how to extract the seeds of cereal grasses for food. They used stones to crush the grain into a coarse flour and made primitive forms of bread. News of the new wonder-food spread, encouraging people in many parts of the Middle East to collect seed, to cultivate land in which to plant it, and to devise ingenious ways of turning the grain into flour. Modern cereals, descended from those ancient grasses, now supply the world not just with bread but with a whole shopping list of items from breakfast cereals to pasta, and even confectionery and beer.

HARVEST CUSTOMS
Traditionally, corn dollies were plaited from the last stalks of the harvest to preserve the "spirit of the corn" – believed to have taken refuge there.

THE DAILY GRIND
In the ancient world, people had to make their own bread. This Greek woman of about 450 B.C. is crushing grain over a block. The flour falls from the block into the basin beneath.

CEREAL SUCCESS STORY
Bread wheat has become the most widely planted of wheat varieties. The large grains, rich in gluten (a kind of protein), produce light, airy bread. Another widely cultivated variety of wheat is durum wheat, from which pasta is made.

Oats   Rye   Barley

STILL GROWING STRONG
Today's major cereals – wheat, barley, oats, and rye – are all descended from wild grasses. Recently, scientists have produced genetically modified varieties to boost harvests. Such wheat can now produce three times more grain than wheat planted in the 1950s.

ROLLING STONES
Stones were used to mill (grind) grain into flour until the coming of iron rollers in the 1700s. Millstones came in pairs. The upper, "runner" stone was turned against a fixed lower stone, called the "bedstone", either by hand, or by animal power, or on a shaft driven by a watermill or windmill. Mills could spin the runner stone – which weighed up to 1.5 tonnes – 200 times a minute. Millstones were typically 1.3 m (4 ft) in diameter and 0.4 m (1.3 ft) thick. This one is made of several pieces of stone held together by a metal band.

Shaft fits into central hole in millstone called the "eye"

In order to carry flour out to edge, millstones' working surfaces carved with furrows (very worn away here), and lower stone slopes down from centre

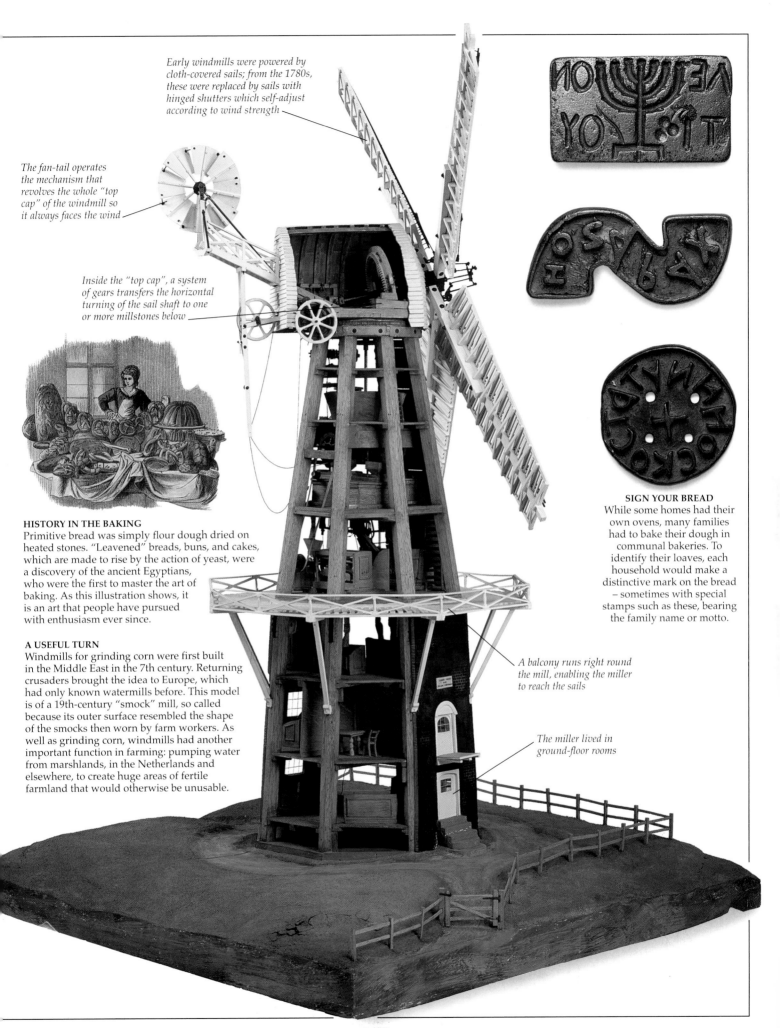

Early windmills were powered by cloth-covered sails; from the 1780s, these were replaced by sails with hinged shutters which self-adjust according to wind strength

The fan-tail operates the mechanism that revolves the whole "top cap" of the windmill so it always faces the wind

Inside the "top cap", a system of gears transfers the horizontal turning of the sail shaft to one or more millstones below

HISTORY IN THE BAKING
Primitive bread was simply flour dough dried on heated stones. "Leavened" breads, buns, and cakes, which are made to rise by the action of yeast, were a discovery of the ancient Egyptians, who were the first to master the art of baking. As this illustration shows, it is an art that people have pursued with enthusiasm ever since.

A USEFUL TURN
Windmills for grinding corn were first built in the Middle East in the 7th century. Returning crusaders brought the idea to Europe, which had only known watermills before. This model is of a 19th-century "smock" mill, so called because its outer surface resembled the shape of the smocks then worn by farm workers. As well as grinding corn, windmills had another important function in farming: pumping water from marshlands, in the Netherlands and elsewhere, to create huge areas of fertile farmland that would otherwise be unusable.

SIGN YOUR BREAD
While some homes had their own ovens, many families had to bake their dough in communal bakeries. To identify their loaves, each household would make a distinctive mark on the bread – sometimes with special stamps such as these, bearing the family name or motto.

A balcony runs right round the mill, enabling the miller to reach the sails

The miller lived in ground-floor rooms

Favourite food

RICE HAS BEEN CULTIVATED by farmers in Asia for at least 7,000 years. A cereal grass, it originally grew wild in India and Australia. Its natural habitat is the tropical flood plain, where heavy rainfall turns the land into a shallow lake for part of each year. To sprout and grow, rice must have water, so farmers imitate the natural conditions it needs by creating "paddy fields" (after the Malay word "padi" meaning rice). Paddy fields have low earth walls or dykes all round them, equipped with sluice gates, into which water can be run from rivers or irrigation channels. They are seen all over Asia, where great numbers of people are still small-scale rice farmers. Rice is now also grown in the United States, southern Europe, and other warm-climate countries. It is said to feed more than half the world's population. Unlike other cereals, it is eaten as a whole grain, although some is ground into flour or used in making beer. Among less well-known uses of the world's biggest harvest is the burning of the husks in which the kernels (the edible grains) grow: the ash from the husks, mixed with lime, makes a very good type of cement!

UNCHANGING WAYS
Many farmers still prepare the ground in the same ways that their ancestors did thousands of years ago. Here the eternal draught animal of Asia, the buffalo, is at work with the harrow.

Seedlings such as this are ready to be moved to their final growing positions

ON THE TERRACES
Water finds its own level, so paddy fields must be made on land that is flat. In hilly regions, farmers ensure a local harvest of rice by cutting into the slopes, forming miniature fields on terraces. This picture is from the Indonesian island of Bali.

These seedlings are 2 days old

IN THE BEGINNING
Traditionally, rice seeds are scattered by hand into flooded seed beds, where they germinate (sprout roots and leaves) underwater.

This seedling is 2–3 weeks old

This seedling is 4–5 weeks old

WET, WET, WET
The roots of the rice plant are constantly flooded during the three- to six-month growing season. After about a month, the seedlings are too crowded in the seed bed. They must be lifted and moved to their final growing positions.

Within two to three weeks the shoot has grown above water level

Shoot grows rapidly

The roots have sprouted

Root still small

Women stoop to press the roots of the young plants into the soft mud of the flooded field

SOFT MUD, HARD WORK
Transplanting rice is a time-consuming and back-breaking task, traditionally done by women in Asian countries, as here in India.

DAILY MEAL

Rice is cooked by boiling, steaming, or frying. In East Asian nations it is eaten by most people every day. Rice contains protein, carbohydrate, and many vital nutrients. Brown rice is the whole grain, minus the gold-coloured husk (protective skin) in which it ripens. White rice is given its bright, shiny look by "polishing" brown rice in machines which remove all traces of the husk (and much nutritional value).

This plant is 3 months old and growing fast

RIPE FOR HARVEST

After three to six months, the heads of the plants begin to droop with the weight of the grains, and the rice is nearly ready for harvest. The water is drained off, and then the ground takes about two weeks to dry off enough for the reapers to begin work. In many parts of Asia, the stalks are still cut with sickles, as they always have been.

Rice grains are naturally golden in colour

Each grain is wrapped in its own husk

RIPENING

Just before the harvest, the water is drained away. The muddy paddy field dries out, and the rice stalks are cut just above ground level.

MACHINE METHODS

Where rice is cultivated in large fields, harvesting can be carried out using combine harvesters, as on this Californian farm. On some big American rice farms the rice is planted by sprinkling it from aircraft.

SEPARATION TIME

Like other cereals, rice must be threshed to separate the edible grain from the straw and husks. In Asia, this is still often done by hand. The husks are used for animal feed and fertilizer, the straw for weaving and for making roofing material.

These Thai farmworkers are beating the cut stalks in a huge woven basket

Maize and potatoes

NATIVE AMERICANS were the first people to grow maize and potatoes, which are both now major crops in much of the world. European settlers in North America called maize "Indian corn", and it is still known there as corn. The huge farms of the midwestern United States produce about half the world's crop, but it is also a major cereal in Brazil, southern Africa, and parts of Asia. New cold-weather varieties are increasingly grown in Europe. Most maize today is grown for animal feed, but it is also used for cooking oil – and those worldwide favourites, cornflakes and popcorn. The humble potato is easy to cultivate even in regions with a cold, wet climate. In the past it has been ravaged by blights and diseases, so potatoes are now bred to be disease-resistant. Today, some potato varieties are specially developed to produce the best potato crisps, chips, or other specialized food products.

TALL STALKS
Some types of maize plant grow to more than 3 m (10 ft) tall. The female flowers bud into corn cobs once they have been fertilized by the airborne pollen of the male flowers at the top of the plant.

LONG HISTORY
Native Americans were cultivating maize, or Indian corn, as early as 6000 B.C. It first became known to the rest of the world when Christopher Columbus, the Italian adventurer, took plants back to Europe, a mere 500 years ago.

On the plant, the cob is covered by a leafy sheath called the husk, here pulled back

Forage-harvester gathers stalks, chops up stems, leaves, and heads of corn, and blows the mixture into the trailer

HEAVY HARVEST
Most maize is grown as a crop for animal feed. The harvest – as much as 75 tonnes for a single hectare (30 tons an acre) – is stored as winter food for livestock.

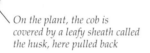

Long handles for easier steering

Some maize has multicoloured grains, black and red as well as yellow

ON THE COB
The harvested cobs above show how the green husks dry to a paper-like texture, revealing the ripe grains – here multicoloured, but usually a brilliant yellow. Some maize varieties have particularly sweet grains, and these are farmed for sale freshly harvested as "corn on the cob" – delicious cooked and served with butter – and for canning or freezing. New varieties can be grown in cooler areas, such as southern Britain, where sweetcorn has become a popular "pick your own" crop.

STOREHOUSES
Maize is stored just like other cereals, in granaries built clear of the ground to keep out both rising damp and hungry rats and mice. These storehouses are in Zambia.

Flowers are white, yellow, or purple

Foliage is tender, and can be damaged by frosts

Tractors collect the sheeting onto a reel once the danger of frosts has passed

The stem of the plant grows to between 30 and 90 cm (1–3 ft) high

SAFE FROM FROST
"Early" potatoes planted in winter are ready for harvest in spring and summer. The young plants can be damaged by frosts, so farmers protect them with a covering of clear plastic sheet. Early potatoes are a valuable crop, fetching higher prices in the shops than the main crop potatoes harvested in the autumn.

PROGRESS AND THE POTATO
Tractor-drawn machines are now used to plant and to harvest potatoes. Here the harvester digs out the rows, gently depositing the crop on the surface for the farm workers to collect. In just 20 years, modern plant-breeding techniques and farming methods have doubled the size of potato harvests. Some farms can produce 37 tonnes of potatoes per hectare (15 tons per acre).

UP AND DOWN
The potato plant puts out shoots above and below ground. The underground shoots separate from the plant's true roots, and swell in places to form the tubers we know as potatoes. When cultivated, the plants are "earthed up" with soil so that the developing potatoes are not exposed to light.

Space between tines allows loose earth to fall through

The "eyes" of potatoes are leaf buds

BETWEEN THE BARS
A potato "shovel", used for loading the harvest into trailers, looks like a fork but has a blunt end to prevent damage to the delicate tubers.

GOOD DIGGER
The potato-raising plough was one of the first implements to speed up the laborious business of lifting the crop. Pulled by a horse team along the banked-up rows, it cut into the ground beneath the plants' roots, lifted the potatoes to the surface, and allowed the soil to fall through the spaces between the tines before depositing the harvest on the ground.

Prongs would pierce the potatoes, so the shovel has a closed end

Potato-raising plough

The rising tines (prongs) lifted the potatoes to the surface

The plough's share (horizontal blade) cut into the ground beneath the plants' roots

Feeding the animals

Kale (above) and turnips (below) are grown for both animals and people

FARMERS FIRST FOUND WAYS of feeding their animals all the year round in Britain in the 1700s. Until then most animals had to be slaughtered when the growing season ended and all the grass was consumed. Otherwise, they would have starved. Only the few animals needed for breeding stock could be fed. When farmers began to grow crops such as the turnip for winter feed, on a large scale, the situation was transformed. Much larger herds could be maintained. From Britain the new ways of farming spread around the world. Today animal feed is big business, but many farmers continue to produce their own, making silage, and growing hay and a wide range of root and leaf crops to feed their animals. In many countries as much as half the cereal harvest is used for animal feed.

NOTHING WASTED
Straw makes a comfortable and easily renewable bedding for livestock in winter. The animals enrich the straw with manure, and afterwards it is spread on the fields and ploughed in as a valuable fertiliser. In the past, fresh straw was also commonly cut up into short lengths to provide winter fodder.

Turnips were loaded into the hopper and cut up small

FOOD PROCESSOR FOR FARMS
Succulent and nutritious, but hard even on the strongest jaws and teeth, bulky winter rootcrops such as turnips can choke hungry animals if fed to them whole. From the 1830s, machines made the hard work of chopping up the vegetables very much easier. They were particularly used for preparing fodder for sheep.

Horse rakes could be up to 5.5 m (18 ft) across

Early root cutters were turned by hand, later ones by steam and electric power

FEEDING THE FOUR-FOOTED
Machines such as this one were used to cut up turnips, potatoes, mangolds, swedes (as here), and other vegetables used for animal feed.

MAKING HAY WHILE THE SUN SHINES

The traditional winter food for livestock for centuries, hay is simply grass – wild or specially planted – which is cut in the heat of summer and left to dry for several days before baling and storing. Even with modern weather forecasting and mechanized collection, many farmers today avoid haymaking because of the risk of rain. When hay was cut with scythes and collected by horse and cart, farmers simply had to trust the weather – and their instincts.

NEVER MIND THE WEATHER

Instead of hay, farmers can make silage for fodder (animal food). The grass is mown in the same way, but instead of being left on the ground to dry it is immediately compressed and sealed up from the air to keep it green. It might be stored in a silo (a covered pit or container) or, as can commonly be seen in the fields in early summer, wrapped in airtight, weatherproof, black plastic sheeting. It smells so awful that it is hard to remember that it is actually nutrititious.

RAKE'S PROGRESS

The horse rake, an invention of the 1800s, could collect eight times as much hay as one hand raker. The hinged steel prongs scooped up a great quantity of hay, and at the field's edge were then raised up by a lever to deposit the load in a long "windrow". This was so called because the wind blew through it, speeding up the vital drying process.

A MEAL FIT FOR A PIG

Known long ago to the ancient Greeks and Romans, turnips have been grown by European farmers for centuries, not just as winter fodder, but also as a supplement to grass and hay for fattening cattle, sheep, and pigs. Other root crops, such as mangolds and swedes, are also frequently used.

Driver sat here and used the lever by his hand to raise and lower the tines

Curved steel prongs, or tines, were hinged to release the hay load

Market gardening

VERSATILE VEGETABLE
Beans are a major market-garden vegetable crop, as well as being an important source of animal feed. Main varieties include navy beans (used for baked beans), runner beans (above), French beans, and broad beans.

NO SOIL TO BE SEEN
Modern farmers can now create "artificial climates" using greenhouses, polythene tunnels, and "hydroponics" (above) by which plants are grown without soil: their roots stand in a liquid solution which contains the nutrients they need to grow.

SMALL-SCALE, SPECIALIZED FARMS known as market gardens have always existed on the edges of towns and cities to provide vegetables, fruit, salad crops, and flowers on a local basis. The public parks of great cities often started life as market gardens – including both Hyde Park and St James's Park in London, England. Today these farms remain an important source of fresh food, and also supply specialized crops to the canning and frozen-food industries. Thanks to the refrigerator and the aeroplane, they can now also deliver their more expensive products, still fresh, to the other side of the world. They often use traditional methods of agriculture that have mostly disappeared from today's very large farms. Some prefer not to use synthetic (human-made) fertilizers or chemicals to combat diseases and pests, preferring to use only organic (natural) means of producing crops.

ORGANICALLY GROWN CAULIFLOWER
Organic farming is kinder to the environment, but it yields smaller harvests. It produces healthier but more expensive food.

THE HUMAN TOUCH
Some crops are still harvested by hand. Mechanical harvesting would damage these globe artichoke plants. They are then steeped in salty water to expel the earwigs which love them, before being boiled and eaten leaf by leaf.

GREENHOUSE EFFECT
Greenhouses (hothouses) enable market gardeners to produce crops out of season, when they fetch much higher prices.

Farmers harvest onions when the green stalks start to wither

Small "cherry" tomatoes, popular for salads

Very broad wooden handle to help farmer to twist dibbler into ground

Carrot leaves were once used in flower arranging and to adorn women's hats

TRAFFIC-LIGHT FRUIT
Tomatoes (a fruit, not a vegetable) are often picked while green; they ripen and go red on their way to the shops.

Peas in the pod

COOKS' CHOICE
Onions have been cultivated from the earliest times, and are grown in most parts of the world. The ancient Egyptians thought they were holy and cooks today take them almost as seriously.

STILL DIBBLING
Most seed is sown by machine but some small farmers still use traditional dibblers for planting vegetable seeds or bulbs one by one, or transplanting crops such as leeks.

Sturdy, heavy metal head

Digger pushes down with foot here

Most market gardeners sell fresh peas still in the pod

Dutch pea pickers at work, c. 1900

Tine

COLOURFUL STORY
Orange carrots were first produced by Dutch farmers in the Middle Ages from two earlier species, one yellow and one purple.

LIFTER
This lifter is a traditional tool for harvesting parsnips and other root crops. It is pushed into the soil so that the two tines pass either side of the root to lift it from below.

WINDLESS FRUIT
Aubergines were first grown in tropical Asia – they were valued for not causing wind when eaten (unlike beans). They are known in North America as egg plants.

THE GOOD OLD DAYS
Some peas are still picked by hand, but peas for freezing are harvested by machines called pea viners, which cut the whole pea vine, remove the pods, and pop out the peas.

Fruit farming

FRUIT IS FARMED worldwide, and fruit growing is a scientific business. For example, more than 6,000 different apple varieties have been created from the original wild apple, and the trees have even been bred to grow so short that pickers don't need ladders! Citrus fruits (oranges, lemons, grapefruits, and limes) grow in warm countries such as Spain, Israel, and South Africa, while apples, pears, and "soft" fruits such as raspberries and strawberries flourish in wetter, cooler regions. Exotic fruits, including bananas and pineapples, come from tropical and sub-tropical regions such as the West Indies and the islands of the Pacific and Indian oceans. Farmers are able to provide fresh fruit to every part of the world, all year round.

FURRY FRIEND
First found growing wild in China and Japan, the peach is now also farmed in Europe, Australia, the United States, and elsewhere. It is related to the almond, cherry, and plum.

PRICKLY CARPET
Shaped like oversized pine cones, pineapples grow up from the ground on short stems. They are cultivated in many different tropical countries.

The sweet orange was first cultivated by the Chinese

Limes, rich in vitamin C

Orange orchard in blossom

Bananas are cut while green and ripen on the way to market

BENDY FRUIT
Bananas don't grow on trees. They grow on the stems of large plants (not trees) in bunches up to 50 kg (110 lb) in weight.

CITRUS STORY
Citrus fruits are cultivated in many warm countries. Because of differing seasons worldwide, there are harvests at most times of the year. The orange orchard below is seen in spring, with the blossom in bloom. The fruit grows on compact trees with dark-green glossy leaves. A single orange tree can produce 1,000 fruits annually for 70 or more years.

Russet
apple

*The russet is a
coarse-skinned apple
of renowned flavour*

*Apples are bred for
sweetness, colour,
and resistance to
disease and pests*

Tasty
pear

WELL BRED
Apple growers have been
developing new varieties
of the world's favourite fruit
for more than 2,000 years.
Most apples are "dessert"
varieties for eating, others are
for cooking or cider-making.

LONG LIFE
Pears are related to
apples, but pear trees
grow taller and more
upright than apple trees
– and last longer, too. As
one country saying has
it, "Who sets an apple
tree may live to see it
end; who sets a pear tree
may set it for a friend".

*Pickers carry the grapes to
carts or trailers in baskets; it's
a traditional method dating
back thousands of years*

*Grapes are usually
picked by hand*

BEES DO IT
Apple breeds are
developed by dusting pollen
from the blossom of one tree on
to that of another – just as bees
do. The fruit from that "crossing"
will bear seeds with the genetic
material of both tree varieties.

The Worcester
Pearmain apple

ON THE GRAPEVINE
Grapes have been cultivated
longer than any other fruit. Piles
of pips up to 7,000 years old have
been found in Turkey. Grapes
were probably first cultivated for
winemaking, and the fruit of the
vine has been ending up as wine
ever since, as well as being eaten
at table. They can be grown in all
but the coldest climates.

Raspberries

Redcurrants

Gooseberries

PLEASURABLE PICKINGS
Soft fruits are cultivated on a
small scale, often on "Pick Your
Own" farms where families can
enjoy a day out in the open – as
well as the fruits of their labours.

Farmhouse and farmyard

Until about 500 years ago, most farms had just one building. Often it was a single-storey structure: the farmer and his family lived at one end, and the livestock lived at the other. In the earliest times, there was no partition between the two halves. Other farmhouses had two floors; the animals were kept below and the family lived upstairs. This helped keep everyone warm at night, although the smell must have been interesting! When extra buildings were constructed, they were built close together to create sheltered yards. Pigs and poultry lived near the house, as they were fed on leftovers, or waste from butter and cheesemaking. Horses were often stabled at the eastern end of the yard, where the farmer would have the benefit of the first light of dawn when hitching up the team to begin the day's work.

PLACE OF SAFETY
Animals such as chickens, geese, and young calves could be kept in the farmyard, safe from predators and from straying thanks to the walls and gates on every side. In this romanticized picture, chickens and geese hurry to be fed, while young calves feed on vegetable leaves.

Steps to granary above cart shed

Water taken from pond to drinking troughs in a horse-drawn tank

Pig sties – covered pens with small open runs

The stable has a hayloft above and a "chaff house" to the side (chaff was grain waste or chopped hay for feeding to horses)

"Nag stable" for the farmer's riding horse

In concrete vacuum towers, air is pumped out to compress the feed into the space available

Cow shed where cows are tied up in stalls for milking

SILOS
Silos for storing animal feed in moist conditions are a common sight on the large livestock farms of today. Silos may be underground pits as well as tall towers.

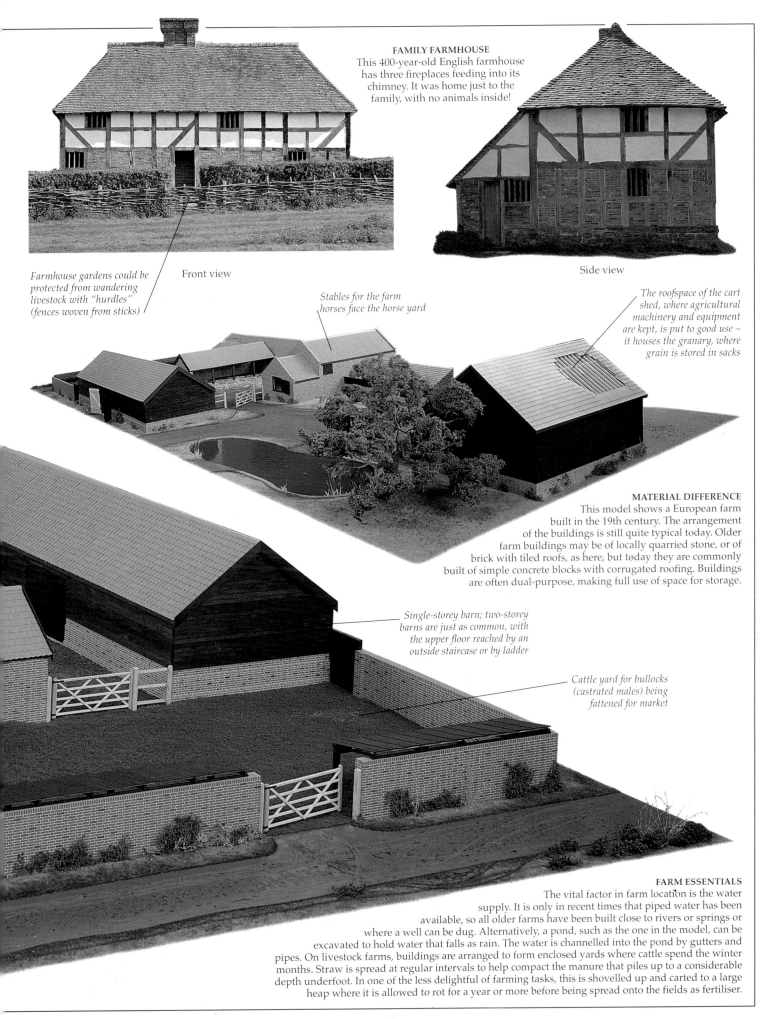

FAMILY FARMHOUSE
This 400-year-old English farmhouse has three fireplaces feeding into its chimney. It was home just to the family, with no animals inside!

Farmhouse gardens could be protected from wandering livestock with "hurdles" (fences woven from sticks)

Front view

Side view

Stables for the farm horses face the horse yard

The roofspace of the cart shed, where agricultural machinery and equipment are kept, is put to good use – it houses the granary, where grain is stored in sacks

MATERIAL DIFFERENCE
This model shows a European farm built in the 19th century. The arrangement of the buildings is still quite typical today. Older farm buildings may be of locally quarried stone, or of brick with tiled roofs, as here, but today they are commonly built of simple concrete blocks with corrugated roofing. Buildings are often dual-purpose, making full use of space for storage.

Single-storey barn; two-storey barns are just as common, with the upper floor reached by an outside staircase or by ladder

Cattle yard for bullocks (castrated males) being fattened for market

FARM ESSENTIALS
The vital factor in farm location is the water supply. It is only in recent times that piped water has been available, so all older farms have been built close to rivers or springs or where a well can be dug. Alternatively, a pond, such as the one in the model, can be excavated to hold water that falls as rain. The water is channelled into the pond by gutters and pipes. On livestock farms, buildings are arranged to form enclosed yards where cattle spend the winter months. Straw is spread at regular intervals to help compact the manure that piles up to a considerable depth underfoot. In one of the less delightful of farming tasks, this is shovelled up and carted to a large heap where it is allowed to rot for a year or more before being spread onto the fields as fertiliser.

Barns and outbuildings

Before the days of concrete blocks and corrugated roofing, farm buildings were often very beautiful. Barns and sheds for sheltering livestock and for storing valuable harvests – and the latest agricultural implements – were elaborately made. They often had oak and elm frames, and beautifully thatched or tiled roofs. There were many ingenious touches. In grain stores, for example, farmers would cut entrance holes near the roof to encourage barn owls to nest there; the birds would prey on the rats and mice that infested all food stores. Today, such buildings are things of the past. Wheat is no longer stored in barns for threshing, and the hay that was once kept there in great quantities has been largely displaced by other fodder crops. The barns that have survived – many of them centuries old – are now used to store farm machinery or have been converted into private houses. A few have been put to educational use as features of museums dedicated to rural history (the history of the countryside).

NOT CHURCHES
Grain is valuable, and these granaries in the Minho region of northern Portugal are not unusual in bearing a cross as a symbol of gratitude for the harvest. The granaries are raised on mushroom-shaped stones to keep out rats and mice.

The space above the hay allowed air to circulate, reducing the risk of it rotting

These upright timbers are called studs

TALL STORAGE
Today's storage buildings include tall towers or "silos" for silage and other feedstuffs for livestock. Grain is also kept in silos, once it has been dried to the right level.

LONG LIFE CROP
Millet is an important grain crop in parts of Asia and Africa where there is insufficient rain to support other cereals. It can be stored for years at a time as a back-up food supply should other crops fail. These earthenware millet granaries are in Niger, in West Africa.

Food stores must be secure against rats

Roof thatch was made of straw from the grain harvest

Tiled roofs were expensive, but lasted much longer than thatch, and were less of a fire risk

Staddle stones raise granary above damp and rats

ONE PURPOSE
This English granary dates from 1731 and consists of a hardwood frame infilled with brick topped by a splendid thatched roof. These granaries were later replaced by combination buildings in which carts were kept on the ground floor and the grain in the loft above. This still kept the grain dry – and the vermin at bay – and made it a simple task to load grain into carts for market.

WELL VENTILATED
This hay barn was built in 1595 in England. The open frame allows good air circulation and lessens the risk of the hay rotting. The barn has just one entrance, so it would not have been used for winnowing, which needed doorways at either end to give a through draught. Timber-framed buildings like this one were often infilled with brick, or with wattle-and-daub (sticks plastered over with mud) to create weather-resistant walls.

REVERSIBLE SHEDS
Cart sheds were usually built outside the yard, or backing onto it. They had open fronts or sides, or both, so the carts and wagons could be manoeuvred in and out without too much reversing. The roof and back wall provided as much shelter from the weather as was necessary.

"Purlins", running the length of the building, support the roof rafters

Tie beams hold the two slopes of the roof together, so its weight does not push the walls outwards

The entrance was wide enough for a cart to pass through

The base or "plinth" is of brick

Dairy farming

COWS, LIKE ALL MAMMALS, make milk to feed their young. The dairy cow gives birth to one calf a year and produces milk for about the next ten months provided she is milked regularly, twice or even three times a day. The amount of milk a cow gives each day varies according to breed, but 10–15 litres (18–27 pints) is average. Friesians, the well-known black-and-white breed, are so productive that a Friesian cow can produce 20 times her own weight in milk per year – up to 10,000 litres (18,000 pints)! In this century, milking machines have revolutionized dairy farming. Today, milking 100 or more animals is only profitable if carried out by machine. Dairy herds have become much larger than they were only a few years ago.

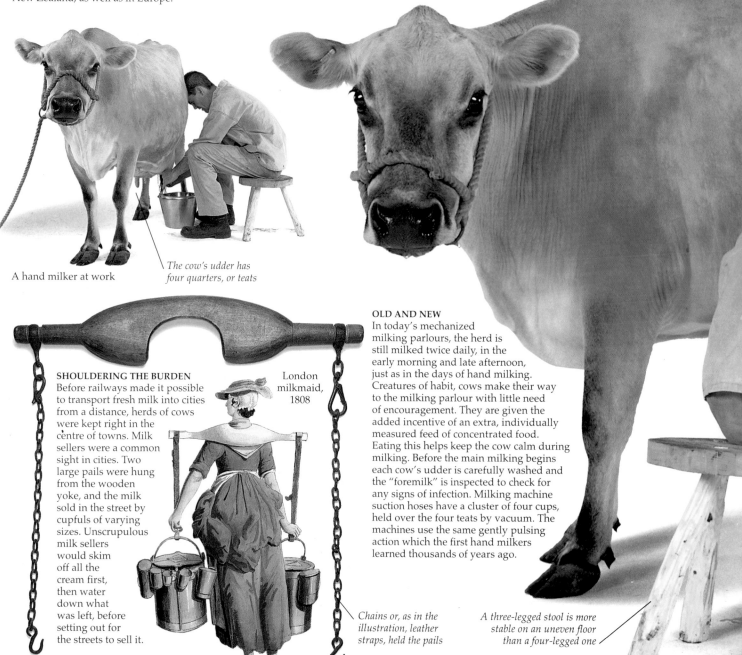

FEEDING TIME
A Jersey cow suckling her calf. These small, delicate cattle have been bred in the Channel Island of Jersey, between Britain and France, since the 1700s. They may be related to a breed farmed by ancient Egyptians. Jersey milk is very rich, with almost 50 per cent more cream than standard milk. Jerseys are widely farmed in North America, Australia, and New Zealand, as well as in Europe.

A hand milker at work

The cow's udder has four quarters, or teats

SHOULDERING THE BURDEN
Before railways made it possible to transport fresh milk into cities from a distance, herds of cows were kept right in the centre of towns. Milk sellers were a common sight in cities. Two large pails were hung from the wooden yoke, and the milk sold in the street by cupfuls of varying sizes. Unscrupulous milk sellers would skim off all the cream first, then water down what was left, before setting out for the streets to sell it.

London milkmaid, 1808

OLD AND NEW
In today's mechanized milking parlours, the herd is still milked twice daily, in the early morning and late afternoon, just as in the days of hand milking. Creatures of habit, cows make their way to the milking parlour with little need of encouragement. They are given the added incentive of an extra, individually measured feed of concentrated food. Eating this helps keep the cow calm during milking. Before the main milking begins each cow's udder is carefully washed and the "foremilk" is inspected to check for any signs of infection. Milking machine suction hoses have a cluster of four cups, held over the four teats by vacuum. The machines use the same gently pulsing action which the first hand milkers learned thousands of years ago.

Chains or, as in the illustration, leather straps, held the pails

A three-legged stool is more stable on an uneven floor than a four-legged one

WHITE COLD TECHNOLOGY
Friesian cows in a modern parlour: during milking, each cow, identified by a brand or ear tag, is given a feed tailored to her needs. A record is kept of the amount of milk she gives. Road tankers collect milk from farms daily.

MILK FOR KIDS
Goats and sheep were kept for their milk long before cattle, and are still farmed for this purpose in many parts of the world. They can thrive on land too dry for cows. Nanny (female) goats usually have twins once a year and give as much as 5 litres (9 pints) of milk a day. Goat's milk is used for making cheese – there are more than a million goats kept in France for this reason – and provides a useful alternative to cow's milk.

A Nubian goat
and her kids

*Milkers use a gentle pulsing action
which mimics the suckling of a calf*

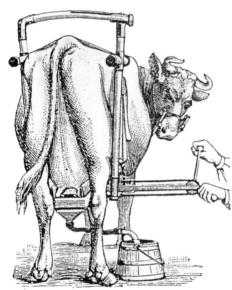

COW AS GUINEA PIG
Early milking machines simply extracted the milk into a pail. This hand-operated Danish contraption of 1892 applied continuous suction rather than the more natural pulsating, suck-pause action always used by calves and hand milkers (and also by today's machines). Small wonder the cow looks aggrieved.

HEALTHY APPETITE
Dairy cows eat a great deal. A large one will eat 70 kg (150 lb) of grass every day – its own weight in grass every week – plus food concentrates. When grass is scarce they are fed hay and silage.

Milk products

FRESH MILK does not stay fresh long, so before the days of modern transport and refrigeration, farmers sold most of this valuable product in preserved form – as butter and cheese. With just a small herd of a dozen cows, a farm could produce 150 litres (265 pints) of milk every day, so the farmer's wife and daughters were kept very busy indeed in the farmhouse dairy. Butter-making does use up a lot of milk: the cream from about 25 litres of milk makes 1 kg of butter (equivalent to 20 pints to 1 lb). In cheese-making, milk is combined with a substance called rennet, to curdle it, and the resulting solid "curd" is then separated from the liquid "whey". The curd is heated and makes the cheese, and the whey is fed to pigs. Today, these activities have mostly been taken over by factories, although farmhouse cheeses and, to a lesser extent, butter are still highly prized in many parts of the world.

YOUR LOCAL MILKMAN
Fresh milk could only be delivered very locally before the days of bulk transport by train began in the later 1800s. This donkey-riding milkman of 1814 is delivering by churn.

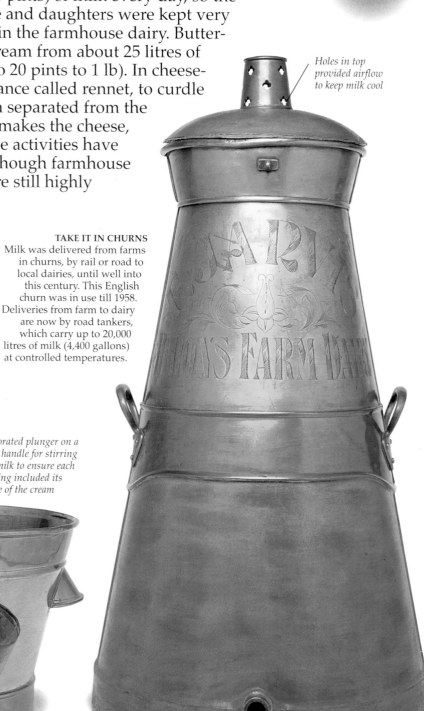

Holes in top provided airflow to keep milk cool

TAKE IT IN CHURNS
Milk was delivered from farms in churns, by rail or road to local dairies, until well into this century. This English churn was in use till 1958. Deliveries from farm to dairy are now by road tankers, which carry up to 20,000 litres of milk (4,400 gallons) at controlled temperatures.

CREAMING IT OFF
Cream is the lightest part of milk, so it naturally settles at the top. A skimmer like this one would be used to remove it from the surface.

Perforated plunger on a long handle for stirring the milk to ensure each serving included its share of the cream

Measuring cups came in different sizes

ON THE COUNTER
"Milk shops" were usually supplied from a town herd. They sold milk from pans such as this one, called "counter pans" because they sat on the shop counter. The milk was carefully stirred before each serving so that all the customers received their rightful share of the cream.

IN THE RIGHT MOULD
To identify the produce of individual farm dairies, butter was traditionally stamped with a patterned mould. The wooden moulds were often very finely carved with agricultural motifs such as the sheaf, wheat ears, and dairy cow illustrated from the left. These moulds date from the 1920s and 1930s. Today they are valued as collector's items.

TERRACOTTA CHEESE
Cheese has been made from the milk of cows and buffaloes, goats and sheep for thousands of years. This terracotta model of a mule with panniers laden with cheeses was probably made as a good-luck token in the hope of good milk yields to come. It was made in Italy in the 3rd or 2nd century B.C.

There were no paddles inside; when the handle was turned the revolving motion was enough to turn the cream into butter

The butter maker thrust this handle up and down

ALL THIS FOR BUTTER
Piston or plunger churns were made from the 1500s. The long handle was attached to a circular paddle, which was thrust up and down inside the cream-filled barrel for half-an-hour or so until the butter solidified. Making butter this way was skilled as well as laborious: the thickness and temperature of the cream had to be just right to make good butter, and as it set, all the remaining liquid (called buttermilk) had to be run off and the butter washed in cold water.

HARD LABOUR
Making butter with a piston or plunger churn was *very* hard work, as the woman in this 1823 illustration seems to be finding.

CREATIVE MOTION
End-over-end churns were invented in about 1750. They were turned by a handle and could turn cream to butter in five to ten minutes – a big improvement on plunger churns. They were the forerunners of the huge churns used in butter-making factories, which have now largely made farmhouse dairies redundant. An alternative way of making butter was provided by barrel-butts, barrels with revolving paddles inside.

The long handle was joined to a circular paddle inside the churn

Solid wooden base

Cattle farming

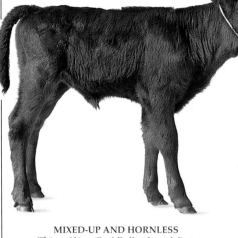

CATTLE WERE ORIGINALLY DOMESTICATED from wild European and Asian species as long as 9,000 years ago. Once they were valued as much for the work they did as draught animals as for their meat and milk. Now they have been succeeded as draught workers in most countries by the horse if not the tractor, but they still provide meat, milk, leather from their hides, fertilizers from their horns and hooves, and other valuable by-products used in medicine and surgery. The country with more cattle than any other is India, with nearly 300 million, mostly descended from the humped Zebu, a breed native to the country. The United States, Argentina, and Australia, all countries with no cattle before the last century, now also have huge herds.

MIXED-UP AND HORNLESS
This calf is a Red Poll, a breed first exhibited in 1862. The word poll in a breed name means that neither cows nor bulls have horns. This is a "dual purpose" breed, bred to provide both meat and milk. It mixes the characteristics of beef cattle – solid and fleshy with wide bodies on short legs – with those of dairy cattle – taller, with long legs and slim, even bony bodies.

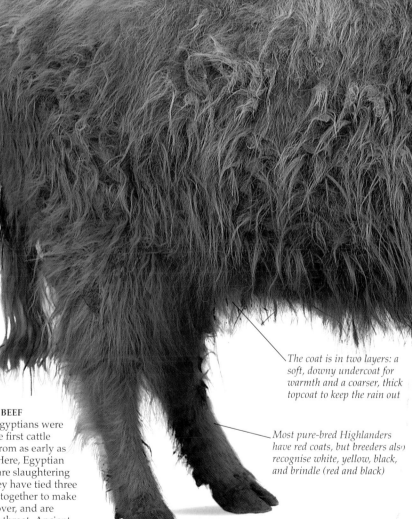

THE CATTLE OF THE WILD WEST
Longhorn cattle were introduced to Mexico from Spain in the 1520s, and arrived in the western United States in the 19th century. Only partly domesticated, they roamed across great expanses of the dry plains in search of grazing. Ranchers and their cowboys had the task of rounding up and driving the herds to market. Longhorns have now been largely replaced in much of the United States by breeds of British origin.

Hair on tail grows down to ground if not trimmed

The coat is in two layers: a soft, downy undercoat for warmth and a coarser, thick topcoat to keep the rain out

Most pure-bred Highlanders have red coats, but breeders also recognise white, yellow, black, and brindle (red and black)

ANCIENT BEEF
Ancient Egyptians were among the first cattle farmers, from as early as 3500 B.C. Here, Egyptian butchers are slaughtering an ox. They have tied three of its legs together to make it topple over, and are cutting its throat. Ancient Egyptians worshipped a bull-god called Apis, and slaughtering the animals had religious associations.

BRED FOR BEEF
The Beef Shorthorn was first bred in England. One bull fetched a world-record price of 1,000 guineas in 1810 and his bones are still on show in the local museum.

NOT A CORKSCREW
This bull tether is screwed down into the ground and the animal is tied to the ring.

ROUND THE WORLD
The Hereford, like many other famous breeds, originated in Britain where, 200 years ago, farmers began to cross-breed systematically to create new breeds that would give more meat. These breeds are now farmed worldwide – Herefords are farmed in 50 countries.

Sharp and widely spread horns

BULL BY THE NOSE
These tongs are put into the nostrils, then locked in position, so the bull can be led by its nose.

STEAK ON THE HOOF
The Aberdeen Angus is known for growing to adult size very rapidly, and for its high-quality meat, which fetches premium prices. Its original breeders came from the Scottish counties of Aberdeenshire and Angus.

SHAGGY COW STORY
Hardy and needing little looking after, Highland cattle have been farmed for their beef since the 16th century on the cold and rain-swept hills of northern Scotland. Enthusiasts still keep them, on a small scale, not just in their native region but in parts of Europe, North America, Australia, and elsewhere. The impressive horns are reminiscent of the horns of the ancient European wild cattle, the aurochs, which were hunted to extinction in 1627. Highland cows are known for being excellent mothers. They can continue to produce calves until they are 16 or 17 years old – much longer than other breeds.

Sheep farming

SHEEP ARE HARDY ENOUGH to survive year-round in the open, and content to be herded with the flock, but they are famously stupid. They also fall prey to many parasites and diseases. Originally domesticated in prehistoric times from the wild sheep of Asia, the first flocks were kept for their skins and for the milk given by the ewes (females). Shearing of sheep followed later. Sheep became more important as a source of meat as people settled in towns and demand for food grew. Farmers learned to cross-breed their animals to provide not just fleeces but larger carcasses. By the 1800s, demand in Europe was such that Europeans set up enormous sheep farms in Australia, New Zealand, and other countries. Today, sheep are farmed around the world. There are dozens of breeds, divided into three groups: longwool (more valued for wool than meat), shortwool (good meat and less wool) and hill breeds (good meat and varying qualities of wool).

Symbol of care: a shepherd holding two lambs

Crook to catch sheep by the neck

SIGN OF THE SHEPHERD
The shepherd's essential tool – and his emblem – is the crook which he uses to catch the sheep, and as an aid to walking in wild country. Invented more than a thousand years ago, the crook was originally all-wood. Iron heads, and sheep-horn ones, followed on later.

"Clucket" bell

RINGS A BELL
To keep track of sheep in open country, bells can be attached to a few sheep. A gentle, steady sound from the bells tells the shepherd where his flock is – a sudden clattering warns of danger.

BOXERS BEWARE
The Lincoln Longwool sheep is a very large breed. Rams (males) weigh up to 140 kg (310 lb) – more than the heaviest heavyweight boxer! First bred in England, breeds throughout the world are descended from it.

Crook to catch sheep by the hind leg; it is smaller than the neck crook

Long fleece is valued for making smooth cloth

TAKING A DIP
Sheep are dipped in a "bath" of protective chemicals to guard against skin parasites, and diseases such as sheep scab. They must be completely immersed for full protection, so the farmer holds each sheep's head below the surface for a few seconds. Most farmers treat their sheep twice a year.

IN A BIG COUNTRY
On the huge farms of Australia, vegetation can be so sparse that one sheep needs as many as 4 hectares (10 acres) to graze, 100 times what is needed per animal on lush pasture. So a single sheep station for a flock of 10,000 may well cover an area of 400 sq km (150 sq miles) – the size of a major city. Farming on this scale calls for shepherding by modern methods, as in this motorcycle round-up of Merino sheep (one of the world's great wool breeds).

Hut contained a bed and an iron stove

Shepherd's only companion was his dog, trained to herd the flock

THE SERVANT OF HIS SHEEP
In the past, shepherds who needed to stay close to their flocks lived in mobile huts. During lambing, when the shepherd might be out on the hillside for weeks at a time, he would set up temporary fencing around the hut, providing shelter and protection for mothers and lambs. Shepherds sometimes nursed sick lambs inside the hut, letting them sleep under the bed.

The Wensleydale is large, hornless, and known for its blue-black head colouring

The Wensleydale and the breeds descended from it are known for high-quality wool

The wool from Greyface Dartmoor sheep is so rough that it is used for rugs and carpets

THE YOUNG ONES
Most lambs are born in the fields in early spring. A few farmers aim to produce them earlier, under shelter. Gestation – the period from conception to birth – is about 150 days. Ewes are bred to produce twins, but many lambs are born singly, some as triplets. A strong new-born lamb is on its feet within minutes, seeking out its mother's udder.

THE OUTLOOK FOR RAMS
Wensleydale rams are often used for crossing with other breeds. Rams can mate with as many as 100 ewes and high-quality rams are much sought after for breeding purposes, while less-promising male lambs are fattened up as fast as possible to make lamb chops. Winter lambs may go to market at ten weeks old, when prices are higher, while spring lambs are fattened during the summer and killed at between three and 15 months.

Sheep shearing

THOUSANDS OF YEARS AGO, farmers killed sheep and removed their hides in order to obtain the valuable wool, to be spun into cloth and knitwear. But since the time of ancient Greece, farmers have sheared sheep for their fleeces (their woolly coats), which the animals then regrow during the following year. Fleeces weigh 2–9 kg (4–20 lb), depending on the breed. Sheep are shorn in summer, usually by shearers who travel from farm to farm with their own electric clippers (rather like the ones used by hairdressers) and can shear each sheep in just over a minute. The world record for shearing is 805 in nine hours – 89 sheep per hour! The sheep on this page was shorn with the hand shears used before machine shearing was introduced in the last century. It took just over five minutes.

Spring-tined shears: the blades spring back into the open position after every cut

1 INTO POSITION
The shearer prepares to shear a Norfolk Horn ewe. He holds the sheep by the fleece at the rump with his hand under her neck so that he can pull her head round and drop her into a sitting position to begin work. Sheep will only sit or lie still if they are on a level surface and firmly but gently held.

3 TURN OVER
With one side complete, the shearer is ready to turn the sheep. He steps over her rear end with his right foot, then, holding her by a horn with his left hand, eases her over on to her left side.

2 SIDE ONE
Kneeling, the shearer arches the sheep across his left leg with her head and shoulders held under his spare arm, positions the shears where the ribs meet, and starts snipping. On a breed such as this, he cuts off the belly wool separately (on some breeds he might keep it with the rest). Then he works all down one side, running the shears up through the neck wool, over the shoulder and flank, and down to the leg.

The sheep is shorn in two stages, either side of the spine

The shears are pointed to get a starting point in the fleece

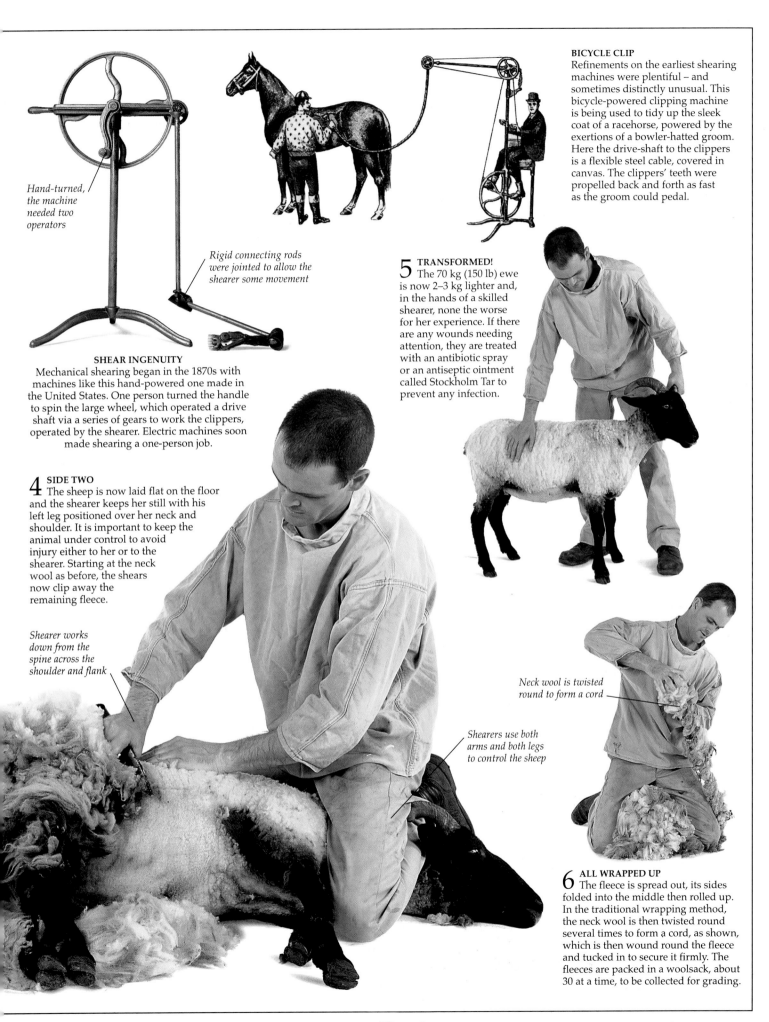

Hand-turned, the machine needed two operators

Rigid connecting rods were jointed to allow the shearer some movement

BICYCLE CLIP
Refinements on the earliest shearing machines were plentiful – and sometimes distinctly unusual. This bicycle-powered clipping machine is being used to tidy up the sleek coat of a racehorse, powered by the exertions of a bowler-hatted groom. Here the drive-shaft to the clippers is a flexible steel cable, covered in canvas. The clippers' teeth were propelled back and forth as fast as the groom could pedal.

SHEAR INGENUITY
Mechanical shearing began in the 1870s with machines like this hand-powered one made in the United States. One person turned the handle to spin the large wheel, which operated a drive shaft via a series of gears to work the clippers, operated by the shearer. Electric machines soon made shearing a one-person job.

5 TRANSFORMED!
The 70 kg (150 lb) ewe is now 2–3 kg lighter and, in the hands of a skilled shearer, none the worse for her experience. If there are any wounds needing attention, they are treated with an antibiotic spray or an antiseptic ointment called Stockholm Tar to prevent any infection.

4 SIDE TWO
The sheep is now laid flat on the floor and the shearer keeps her still with his left leg positioned over her neck and shoulder. It is important to keep the animal under control to avoid injury either to her or to the shearer. Starting at the neck wool as before, the shears now clip away the remaining fleece.

Shearer works down from the spine across the shoulder and flank

Shearers use both arms and both legs to control the sheep

Neck wool is twisted round to form a cord

6 ALL WRAPPED UP
The fleece is spread out, its sides folded into the middle then rolled up. In the traditional wrapping method, the neck wool is then twisted round several times to form a cord, as shown, which is then wound round the fleece and tucked in to secure it firmly. The fleeces are packed in a woolsack, about 30 at a time, to be collected for grading.

Goat farming

GOATS EAT JUST ABOUT ANYTHING. It's the secret of their success. They can eat much shorter grass than sheep and will happily consume brambles and thistles. Some resemble sheep, but can always be told apart because the billies (males) have beards, and at times give off a horrible smell. They were probably first tamed by farmers in the Middle East, perhaps 10,000 years ago. European breeds are kept mainly for their milk, used for making fine cheeses, yogurt – and chocolate. Eastern or Nubian goats are farmed in Asia for both milk and meat. Wool goats, such as the Angora and Cashmere, are bred in many parts of the world, mainly for their fleeces.

NO END TO THEIR APPETITE
If not controlled, goats can seriously damage the landscape. On the Mediterranean island of Cyprus, where this flock is following the goatherd, goats once destroyed whole forests.

Goats of both sexes have horns, unlike sheep

GOLDEN WONDER
The handsome Golden Guernsey is known for its docile and friendly nature – not something goats are famous for. This breed was first recorded on the island of Guernsey in 1826, but its ancestors are believed to be wild goats from France, Syria, and Malta. The Golden Guernsey is quite a small breed. On average, nanny (female) goats produce two kids (young) as twins each year over a span of eight years.

SWISS KIDS
A Saanen (left) and a Saanen-Toggenburg cross; both breeds come from Switzerland.

Adult males weigh about 70 kg (150 lb), females 50 kg (110 lb)

SMALL IS BEAUTIFUL
Pygmy goats belong to the wool group of breeds. This compact "dwarf" breed originates from equatorial Africa and these goats are still widely kept in the region. They come in all colours except pure white. North Africa is the centre of the goatskin trade, producing leather known as Morocco or kidskin.

A Golden Guernsey's coat may be long or short

HIGH TABLE
Accustomed to living on the steepest mountainsides and always willing to go the distance for the unlikeliest titbit, goats are agile and determined climbers. In search of spiky greenery that few other animals would relish, this one has found its way into the upper branches of a thorn tree in northern Kenya.

THE EARS TELL
Saanens belong to the European group of breeds, originating in Switzerland and now farmed around the Continent. They have upright ears, unlike eastern breeds with their long, floppy ones.

Female Saanens are renowned for their milk, producing about 3,000 litres (5,000 pints) a year

The horns of male goats are larger than those of females

Angoras have two kinds of hair, a coarse undercoat and a long, curly wool outer coat, which provides some of the world's most valuable wool

Coats come in all shades of gold, sometimes with white markings

The fleece from a fully grown adult can weigh up to 7kg (15lb)

WEAR WITH PRIDE
The Angora came originally from near Ankara, Turkey, and is now farmed in places as far apart as Alaska and New Zealand. Angora wool is woven into a fine cloth called mohair.

Pig farming

IN THEIR WILD STATE, pigs are forest animals. Until the late 18th century, they were grazed in woodland, still semi-wild, finding their own food, digging up roots and grubs with their snouts as well eating from the surface. Only when sows (females) were ready to have piglets would they be brought to shelter in sties (pigpens). Today, pig farmers usually keep pigs in covered units, although some pigs still live in open fields, with "arks" (movable shelters) to protect them from the weather. Most are bred to grow quickly and produce lean meat.

Fully grown boars (males) of the commonest breed, the Large White, weigh 500 kg (half a ton). Pigs happily eat cereals, vegetable crops, and by-products from milking or even brewing. They provide us with pork, bacon, sausagemeat, and ham, their skins are used for leather, their bristly hair for brushes, and their organs for life-saving medical substances.

FREEDOM-LOVING SWINE
In medieval times, pigs lived in orchards or open woodland. Herds were looked after by a "swineherd" in the same way that a shepherd looks after sheep.

LOOKS AREN'T EVERYTHING
Vietnamese Pot-bellied pigs are not famous for their good looks, but this tiny, docile breed is popular with small farmers in many parts of the world.

FAMILY BUTCHER
Before large-scale pig farming, many country people kept a single pig at home and killed it themselves for food.

WILD PAST
Modern farm breeds were created by crossing European pigs with Southeast Asian ones. The hardy Tamworth (right) may have originated partly from a red-coloured jungle boar from India in about 1800. It looks rather like the wild pig of early times.

Purebred Tamworths such as this sow are now rare

POPULAR PORKERS
The British Saddleback is a large breed valued for its ability to forage for its own food. A new breed itself, dating only to 1966, the Saddleback is often crossed with other breeds to produce animals that will thrive outdoors in open-field pig farms, now increasingly popular again. Saddlebacks are also known for being good-tempered and easy to handle. This sow is with one of her piglets, now aged 12 weeks and weaned off milk two months ago. Depending on the breed, sows can give birth to as many as 20 piglets at a time (ten is average), and they can do it twice a year. New-born piglets only weigh about 1.5 kg (3 lb) at birth but can reach 100 kg (220 lb) in less than six months.

SNUFFLE THAT TRUFFLE
Farmers train pigs to find (and not to eat) the much-prized fungi called truffles, a costly luxury food found in regions such as Périgord in France.

The Gloucester
Old Spot

STAR PIG
Pigs such as this Middle White were, and are, stars of livestock shows at which farmers choose new breeding stock.

A PIG FOR ALL SEASONS
There is an old country saying: "There's no part of a pig that can't be put to good use – except its squeal." Pigs are versatile feeders too. The Gloucester Old Spot (or Spots) was once called the orchard pig, because it lived on windfall apples – fruit that fell from the trees before picking time. It is an "all-purpose" pig, producing young suitable for either being killed early for pork or kept longer for bacon and other meat products.

The name Saddleback comes from the white band that runs across the animal's back and right round the body

Lop ears cover the eyes

Sows have many teats – for feeding litters of up to 20 piglets

"Trotters" (pigs' feet) have four toes, the inner pair much larger than the outer, and a distinct heel

THE EMPEROR'S CHICKENS

Pekin bantams were brought to Europe from the Summer Palace of the Chinese Emperor in Peking (now Beijing). Bantams are bred to be small. Some are exact miniatures of the birds they are bred from, but a quarter as heavy.

Chicken farming

THE CHICKENS PECK QUIETLY in the farmyard under the watchful eye of the cock, perched proudly on the dung-heap. Occasionally, as he has done since dawn, he throws back his head and crows: "Cock-a-doodle-do!" This is the traditional picture of poultry farming. Some flocks do still live in this way, now known as "free-range" farming. But most of the eggs and chickens in the shops today come from large "factory" farms which process more than 100,000 birds at a time. Today's hens are hybrids, cross-bred to produce more and better eggs and meat. Table birds or "broilers" are hatched in 21 days in huge incubators and the chicks fed scientifically to grow fast for slaughter at about ten weeks old. Laying hens are kept in cages all their lives, which last less than a year. Their eggs – they produce one or more every day – are collected automatically.

Feathery leg and foot plumage is a mark of a Chinese breed called Cochin, which the Pekin bantam resembles

Laying compartments make it easier to find the eggs

Side view of coop

SAFE HOUSE
The coop has hinged shutters that can be closed up at night for warmth, and to keep foxes out.

The "pop hole" enables the birds to get in and out while the door is closed

Front view of coop

Light Sussex chickens

HOME ON THE RANGE
Free-range chickens need a chicken coop, or house, in which to lay and sit on their eggs, where they can be shut in at night, safe from predators such as foxes. It is mounted on wheels so it can be moved to clean ground and fresh pickings. A temporary enclosure or "run" can be made round it with a fence of chicken wire.

58

BREEDER'S TREASURE

Traditional breeds are not kept by big farmers, but have survived thanks to the efforts of enthusiastic poultry breeders in many countries. Old breeds are still used for cross-breeding to create new breeds because they preserve characteristics that today's commercial breeds have lost.

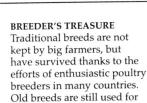

ROYAL CONNECTION

Brahmas, believed originally to be from Brahmaputra in India, became famous and fashionable when an enterprising breeder presented Britain's Queen Victoria with nine of them in 1852 amidst a blaze of publicity. This pair are Dark Brahmas.

Brown egg of Buff Sussex chicken

The fleshy growth on top of the fowl's head is called the comb

The part below the head is known as the wattle

Pale blue egg of Muscovy duck

White egg of Silver-grey Dorking chicken

CROSS BREED

Brought to Europe 200 years ago, Malay birds from southern Asia are up to 80 cm (32 in) tall. Savagely bad-tempered, they were well suited to the cruel sport of cock-fighting, popular until the 1800s.

Buff Sussex chick

Silver-grey Dorking chick

Buff Orpington chicken

BEFORE FACTORY FARMING

Until the modern farming era of the last 50 years, chickens were mostly reared on a small scale in farmyards. They were fed on kitchen scraps and spare grain, along with any seeds, insects, or other morsels they could find in the yard. In return, they gave fresh eggs – though far fewer than today's chickens do.

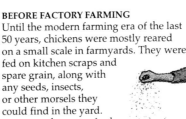

HANDSOME BIRDS

The Orpington breeds of duck and chicken were created in Orpington, England, in the last century. Pure breeds are still used to produce today's hybrid (cross-bred) chickens. One famous cross was that between a Rhode Island Red and a Light Sussex hen, which produced male and female young with different colouring, making the task of identifying the sex of new-born chicks easier.

Ducks and geese

FARMYARD FOWL
For domestic ducks a pond or river is an option rather than a necessity. They like to forage for their food, eating grass and weeds and digging up worms and grubs, but they need to be kept inside a run at night, both for protection from predators and so they lay their eggs where the eggs can be collected.

German Saxony duck

GRAZING BIRD
Geese are grazing birds, content to eat fresh grass. Most domestic geese descend from the wild Greylag species, including the very first ones to be farmed – in ancient Egypt, at least 4,000 years ago. Other breeds, such as the Chinese (above) descend from the Siberian swan goose.

Chinese gander (male goose)

DUCKS AND GEESE were once more important in farming than they are today. Their down and feathers were plucked up to five times a year and used for bedding, arrow flights, furniture upholstery, and to make quills (the main writing implements until the 1800s) – and they produced meat and eggs as well. In the Middle Ages geese were kept in huge flocks on open land. When ready for market, they were walked to town in their thousands. Gooseherds would dip the birds' feet in tar to protect them for the long journey. Turkeys arrived later: they were first domesticated by Spanish settlers in the Americas in about 1500. At first they were raised and delivered in the same way as geese. As a roast for special occasions they quickly upstaged other birds – swans and peacocks had been farmed for that purpose, as well as geese. Today, turkeys are "factory" farmed in vast units but ducks and geese do not respond well to such conditions and are largely kept as free-range fowl.

FEATHERED GUARD DOG
Geese are known for being fierce, noisy, and unfriendly to strangers. They have a reputation for being good watchdogs that goes back more than 2,000 years. A flock of geese is said to have saved the city of Rome, in Italy, in 390 B.C. Invaders crept into the city at night, but the sleeping guards were alerted by the loud cackling and honking of the geese.

Buff Orpington duck

FARMYARD ADOPTION
Ducks and chickens often share a farmyard. Ducks tend to neglect their eggs, so the farmer may move them to the chicken house, where broody hens will happily sit on them.

THANK THE INCAS
All farmyard ducks descend from the common wild Mallard, except for Muscovies such as this Lavender White. Despite their name, Muscovies originally came not from Russia but from South America, where they were domesticated by the Incas of Peru. They are large ducks and their eggs take 35 days to hatch, a week longer than other breeds' eggs.

Turkeys may get their name from these strange "caruncles"; they resemble the red tassels of the fez hats traditionally worn in Turkey

BORN TO RUN
Runner ducks come originally from India, where they are said to have been first bred 2,000 years ago. They are very upright and scamper rather than waddle, hence the name. Runners lay more eggs than other breeds, as many as 300 a year. The duck and drakes on the right are of a small breed called Trout Runners (the female's colouring is like a trout's).

NOT JUST FOR CHRISTMAS
Turkeys are raised for their meat, all year round, in huge units similar to broiler farms. They are slaughtered at 12–24 weeks old (ducks are killed at eight weeks, chickens at ten). Today's commercial breeds are white, and big. Stags (males) weigh 14 kg (30 lb) or more. British farmyard turkeys of earlier times included the Norfolk Black (above).

WELCOME REFUGE
To encourage ducks and other game onto their land, farmers and gamekeepers put out nesting baskets.

The future of farming

TODAY'S CHICKENS lay twice as many eggs as the chickens of 80 years ago, and 1990s wheat produces three times as much grain as wheat did 40 years ago. Scientific breeding and genetic engineering continue to develop livestock and crops that grow bigger and faster. Advances in veterinary care (animal medicine) and pesticides will keep animals and plants healthier. But with this progress there is a price. Only the most profitable animals and crops are farmed, so other breeds and varieties die out. Some modern farming methods damage the environment badly. As bigger farms use more machines and chemicals, they need fewer human workers – in Europe, there are half as many people working on the land as there were 30 years ago. Here and there people fight against these trends – farmers return to more traditional organic methods, rare breeds of livestock are preserved for future breeding. Meanwhile, in parts of the developing world, farming goes on much as it always has.

FRIEND OR FOE?
Some insects are pests, but most are harmless to crops, or even protect them by preying on their plant-eating cousins. The ladybird is a prime example. Here it is eating aphids, which can ruin fruit and vegetable harvests. In many parts of the world, farmers are now turning away from pesticides – chemicals that destroy weeds, insects, and diseases – because they sometimes harm the environment. Instead, they are trying to use natural means to protect their crops.

Colour of wool ranges from white to a rich chocolate brown

ANCIENT AND MODERN
The Jacob sheep is an ancient breed that was mentioned in the Bible. This ram has two fine horns, but others might have none – or as many as six. The ewes are good mothers and usually produce two or more black-and-white lambs. Jacobs are an example of a traditional breed now coming back into favour. Small-scale farmers are keeping them in growing numbers, for their exceptionally good meat as well as for their wool.

THE VALUE OF TRADITION
To continue "improving" pigs, sheep, and cattle so that new generations are healthier and more productive, breeders need to have access to a wide diversity of existing breeds. Farmers themselves do not usually keep old breeds, and in the past many became extinct. Today "rare breed societies" in many countries ensure that famous breeds such as the Gloucester Old Spot do not die out.

Pigs have sensitive skin (it doesn't have much hair to protect it) so they can easily get sunburnt, and they don't like rain or cold weather either

Pigs can use their powerful snouts to dig up roots and grubs, as well as eating from the surface

Gloucester Old Spot sow

QUALITY NOT QUANTITY

Fifty years after the first factory farms for poultry were started in Europe, free-range chickens are making a comeback. Of the ten billion eggs eaten in Britain each year, ten per cent are free range, bought by people who believe they taste better and come from happier chickens. This is part of a wider move back towards more natural farming methods, which many farmers are now embracing – seeking for quality not quantity, and to be kinder to the environment. It is helped by some scientific developments, particularly those that are breeding more pest- and disease-resistant crops and animals, which make it easier to do without pesticides. Nevertheless, the business of farming is still dominated by the drive to produce more and more, and the main trend is still towards farming on a large, almost industrial scale.

TEST-TUBE BABIES

Using the science of genetics, breeders can "improve" plants. These "test-tube baby" plants have been grown not from seed but from cells taken from a parent plant. The cells are selected to be immune to disease, so the plants are too, and won't need to be sprayed with chemicals to prevent or cure infection.

NATURAL METHODS

Intercropping is an organic method of growing healthy crops without using chemicals. Each crop depends on particular nutrients in the soil, so different ones planted together can both thrive without the need for fertilizers. Here beans – which actually improve the soil – are planted alongside wheat. Intercropping can also protect against pests when crops disliked by certain insects are planted next to those that would normally be attacked by them.

Gloucester Old Spot piglets

Index

A

animal by-products, 6–8, 14, 40, 44–48, 50–56, 58–63
ard, 12
apples, 38, 39

B

Bakewell, John, 7
barley, 6, 21, 22, 26, 28
Bayeux Tapestry, 15
bees, 16, 39
bird deterrent, 18, 19
bread, 28, 29
buffalo, 30, 47
buildings, farm, 20, 23, 32, 35, 40–43, 56
  barn, 20, 23, 41–43
  granary, 32, 40–43
  stables, 40, 41
  sties, 40, 42, 56
butter making, 40, 46, 47

C

camels, 13
canning, 36
carts, 8, 21, 35, 43
Catal Huyuk, 6
cattle, 6–8, 14, 16, 35, 40, 41, 44–49, 62
  Aberdeen Angus, 49
  Friesian, 44, 45
  Highland, 48, 49
  Jersey, 44
cereals, 6, 14, 27, 28, 30, 34
chaff, 22–25
cheese, farmhouse, 46
cheesemaking, 40, 45, 46, 54
chemicals, 18, 19, 36, 62, 63
chickens, 7, 40, 58, 59, 61–63
  cock-fighting, 59
  coop, 58
  "free range", 58, 63
cider-making, 39

clover, 14
  white, 16
  wild, 16
Columbus, Christopher, 32
corn, 8, 20–29, 32
  Indian, 32
cream, 44, 46
crops, 7, 12, 14–19, 27, 32, 39
  rotation, 14
  spraying, 19
cross-breeding, 49, 50, 56, 59, 62
cross pollination, 39
cultivating, 10, 12, 28
cultivators, 13, 15

D E F

dairies, 46, 47
dibbler, 37
dibbling, 16
donkeys, 8, 46
drinking vessels, 6, 7
ducks, 59–61
  Mallard, 61
  Muscovy, 59, 61
eggs, 7, 58–61, 63
equipment, 10, 11, 13
  earth-moving, 10
  hydraulic, 11, 13
factory farms, 58, 60, 63
  broiler farms, 61
farmers, ancient:
  Chinese, 17
  Egyptian, 6, 12, 28, 29, 37, 44, 48, 54, 60
  Greek, 6–8, 28, 35, 52
  Roman, 6, 7, 12, 17, 20, 35, 60
  Stone Age, 6, 8, 14, 20
farmers, early:
  medieval, 56
  Middle Ages, 14, 37, 60
  Saxon, 13
fertiliser, 34, 36, 40, 41, 48, 63
flail, 22–24
fleece, 50, 52–54
flour, 28, 30
fodder, 16, 20, 32, 34–36, 40, 42, 44, 45, 57, 59
forks, 21
  barley, 21
  pitch, 21
Fowler, John, 12
frozen food, 36, 37
fruit, 38, 39

fruit farming, 6, 38, 39, 62

G

geese, 40, 60
genetic engineering, 28, 62, 63
goatherd, 54
goats, 6, 45, 54, 55
  Angora, 54, 55
  Cashmere, 54
  Pygmy, 54
grain, 6, 20–27, 42, 43, 62
  crushing, 28
  grinding, 28
  whole, 28
grasses, 6, 9, 14, 16, 28, 35, 45, 54
  ancient, 28
  wild, 6, 28
grasslands, 16
grazing, 14, 16, 48
greenhouses, 36

H I J

harrows, 8, 9, 13–15, 30
harvester, combine, 24–27, 31
harvester, forage, 32
harvesting, 7, 10, 13, 16, 18, 20–25, 31–34, 36, 42, 43
  gleaning, 20, 21
  rice, 31
  ricks, 20–22
  stack stand, 22
  thatched stacks, 23
hay, 8, 9, 16, 20, 21, 34, 35, 42, 43, 45
hay-making, 20, 35
hoeing machine, 16, 17
horses, 7–10, 13–16, 22, 24, 26, 33–35, 40, 48
  draught, 14
  harness, 9, 14
horsepower, 11
hunter-gatherers, 6, 28
hydroponics, 36
irrigation, 29, 30
Industrial Revolution, 14

K L M N

lifter, vegetable, 37
llamas, 13
maize (corn), 6, 32

"corn on the cob", 32
  sweetcorn, 32
manure, farmyard, 8, 14, 34, 41
market gardening, 36–39
McCormick, Cyrus, 26
meat, 6–8, 14, 48, 50, 51, 54, 56–58, 61, 62
Meikle, Andrew, 24
milk, 6–8, 44–48, 50, 54, 55
  buttermilk, 47
  maids, 47
milking, 44, 45
millet, 6, 42
millstone, 28
mowing, 10, 35
mule, 47
Native Americans, 32

O P

oats, 6, 28
organic farming, 36, 58, 60, 62–63
  "free range", 58, 60
  intercropping, 63
ox, 8, 12–15, 48
pea, 37
  pickers, 37
  viner, 37
peacocks, 60
pests and diseases, 13, 18, 19, 36, 39, 50, 60, 62, 63
  aphids, 19
  birds, 18, 19
  butterflies and moths, 18, 19
  earwigs, 36
  foxes, 58
  insects, 18
  locusts, 19
  rabbits, 18
  resistance to, 62, 63
  rodents, 26, 42, 43
  wildlife, 18
pigs, 7, 35, 40, 46, 56–57, 62, 63
  "arks", 56
  truffles, 57
  Vietnamese Pot-bellied, 56
  wild, 56
ploughs, 8–14, 17, 33
  hydraulic, 13
  wooden, 12
ploughing, 11–14
potatoes, 8, 32–34
  blight, 19

poultry, 7, 40, 58–61, 63

Q R

rake, 21, 23, 34, 35
  drag, 21
  horse-drawn, 34, 35
  thatcher's, 23
ranches, cattle, 48
rapeseed, 14
rare breed societies, 62
reaper-binder, 26, 27
reaper, sail, 26
reaping, 20, 25–27, 31
rice, 6, 30, 31
rollers, 14
  Kit Kat Roll, 14
roofs, 42, 43
  thatched, 42, 43
  tiled, 42, 43
root-cutters, 34
rye, 16, 28

S

scythe, 20, 35
  hook, 20
seed, 7, 8, 15–17, 28, 30
  broadcasting, 7, 16
  collecting, 28
  drills, 8, 15–17
  seed-lip, 17
sheaves, 20, 21, 24, 26
  sheaf-makers, 20, 21, 24
sheep, 6, 7, 16, 34, 35, 45, 50–54, 56, 62
  "clucket bell", 50
  dog, 51
sheep shearing, 6, 7, 50, 52, 53
shepherd, 50, 51, 56
shepherd's crook, 50
sickle, 20, 31
silage, 11, 16, 34, 35, 45
silo, 35
skins, 6, 8, 48, 50, 52, 54, 56
  kidskin, 54
  leather, 48
soil preparation, 12–15, 28
  tilth, 15
  topsoil, 13
sower, hand, 17
sowing, 6, 7, 12, 14, 16–18
  dibbling, 16
sowing machines, 16, 17

spraying, 18, 19
  aerial crop, 19
  chemical, 18, 19
steam engine, 10, 12, 13, 24
straw, 22–24, 34, 41, 43
  for bedding, 34
swans, 60

T U V

threshing, 20, 22–25, 27, 42
tractors, 8–11, 15–17, 19, 26, 33, 48
  Allis-Chalmers, 11
  metal lugwheel, 10
  pneumatic tyres, 11
Tull, Jethro, 16, 17
turkeys, 60, 61
vegetable oil, 14
vegetables, 18, 34, 36, 37, 62
  aubergine, 37
  beans, 36, 63
  cabbage, 18
  cauliflower, 36
  globe artichoke, 36
  kale, 34
  tomatoes, 37
vegetables, root, 8, 9, 14, 16, 18, 32–35, 37
  carrots, 37
  leeks, 37
  mangolds, 34, 35
  onions, 37
  parsnips, 37
  swedes, 34, 35
  turnips, 8, 14, 16, 18, 34

W X Y Z

wagons, 8, 43
watermill, 28, 29
water supply, 40, 41
weather, 20, 27, 33, 35
  "artificial climate, 36
weed control, 13, 18, 19
weedkillers "selective", 19
wheat, 6, 14, 16, 22, 26, 28, 62, 63
windmill, 28, 29
winemaking, 39
winnowing, 22–25, 27, 43
  fan, 23
wool, 52–55, 62
  mohair, 55

Acknowledgements

Dorling Kindersley would like to thank:
Barleylands Farm Museum and Animal Centre (Nick Smith); the British Museum; Chiltern Open Air Museum (Miriam Moir, Chris Turner); Elsoms Seeds Ltd; Fred Hams; Norfolk Museums Service; Norfolk Rural Life Museum and Union Farm (Andrew Mackay, Martin Collier, Richard Dalton); Odds Farm Park (Stephen Vinden, Derek House, Debbie Fenn); the staff of the Royal Botanic Gardens, Kew (David Cooke); Rural History Centre, The University of Reading; South of England Rare Breeds Centre (Margaret Hanlon, Ian Bailey); Suffolk Horse Museum; Weald and Downland Open Air Museum (Bob Powell, Peter Albon).
Design and editorial help:
Susila Baybars, Ivan Finnegan, Mark Haygarth, Joseph Hoyle, Cormac Jordan
Artwork: Sallie Alane Reason

Endpapers: John Woodcock
Index: Marion Dent
Additional photography:
Jon Bouchier (p. 45); Gordon Clayton (p. 2); Andrew McRobb of the Royal Botanic Gardens, Kew (pp. 30–31); Nick Nicholls of the British Museum (pp. 6–7, 28, 47)

Picture credits
(a = above, b = below, c = centre, l = left, r = right, t = top)
Heather Angel: 8al; Bridgeman Art Library, London / Ackermann and Johnson Ltd, London: 61al / Chris Beetles, London: 40ar /British Library, London: 6bcl / Iona Antiques, London: 7al, 49al; British Museum: 6acr; J. L. Charmet: 21al /Bibl. des Arts Décoratifs: 22acr, 23tc, 37bcr, 59br; Bruce Coleman Ltd / John Anthony: 43ar / Mark N. Boulton: 32cb / Eric Crichton: 45br /Dr Sandro Prato: 31br / Michel Viard: 57al; Colorific / Don Rutledge

/Black Star: 56acr; John Deere Ltd: 32cr; Ecoscene / Anthony Cooper: 45al / Kay Hart: 63cr; e.t. archive: 17ar, 32ar /Biblioteca Estense Modena: 20cl /Bibliothèque Nationale, Paris: 16ar, back cover cra /Victoria and Albert Museum: 18br; Mary Evans Picture Library: 12bcl, 13al, 16cl, 20bc, 26bc, 32al, 34ar, 34bc, 35cr, 59tc, 59ar, 59cr; FLPA/E. & D. Hosking: 33cr /Mark Newman: 36cl; Giraudon /Bridgeman Art Library, London / Musée des Beaux-Arts, Nantes: 39br / Musée Condée, Chantilly: 7ar, 56al; Robert Harding Picture Library / David Beatty: 13tcr; Michael Holford: 14–15t; Holt Studios International: 15ar /Richard Anthony: 42bcl /Nigel Cattlin: 31c, 36bcr, 54cl, 63al /P. Karunkaran: 30bl /Inga Spence: 31cr; Hutchison Library / Tony Souter: 11bcr; Image Bank / Barros & Barros: 27al; Images Colour Library: 11ac; Magnum Photos / Guy Le Querrec: 36b; Mansell Collection: 9ar, 17acl, 24c;

NHPA / Anthony Bannister: 62al; Pictor International: 54ar; Ann Ronan at Image Select: 8br, 15br, 17tc, 29acl, 44bl, 46al, 47cr, front cover cr; Rural History Centre, University of Reading: 10ar, 11tl, 14cl, 14br, 18cl, 21bl, 22c, 26ar, 50al, 50bl, 51ar, front cover tr; Science Museum: 29cl; Science Photo Library /Martin Bond: 33ar / Charlotte Raymond: 63ar; Tony Stone Worldwide / Peter Dean: 35ar / Beverly Factor: 38cl / Gary Holscher: 38al / Hilarie Kavanagh: 30cl; Telegraph Colour Library / Jon Arnold: 38b; Zefa Pictures: 25al, 40bl, 42acl, 48cl; APL : 51al / F. Damm: 27ar / T. Lancefield: 55ar /Stockmarket / Russel Munson: 19tr / Tortoli: 19bcl

Every effort has been made to trace the copyright holders of photographs, and we apologize if any omissions have been made.